Christian Transition

Christian Transition

'... even in this world ...
(1 John 4:17)

JOSEPH SHIELS, SSC

Gracewing

First published in 2007

Gracewing
2 Southern Avenue, Leominster
Herefordshire HR6 0QF

Cover photograph: Lough Swilly, looking south west along the Donegal coastline towards Rathmullen © Bernard McCloskey, 2007.

ISBN 978 0 85244 287 6

Typeset by Action Publishing Technology Ltd,
Gloucester GL1 1SP

Printed in England by
Athenaeum Press Ltd, Gateshead NE11 0PZ

Contents

Introduction

Since the beginning of the last century, pope after pope has alerted us to the dangers of secular humanism in all its aspects, ranging from the extremes of Communism and Nazism to the insidiousness of consumerism. As regards its impact on religion, one of the seductive but still lethal outcomes of this secular humanism system of beliefs is that people nowadays have no hesitation in first of all stating their preferences regarding what they want in religion. This is equally true of some Christians.

For this to happen, they must face the problem of the two-thousand-year existence of Christianity, with some of its aspects which they do not like. They then shop around seeking a set of religious or quasi-religious beliefs that suit them.

It can also be faced in two other more extreme ways. One is to ignore Christianity as being irrelevant and not worth any more attention than merely saying so. The other is to do a more thorough job, and undertake the task of rubbishing Christianity in any way possible. We have seen, in the readership of *The Da Vinci Code* novel, the millions of people who wish to follow this last solution to their cognitive dissonance regarding the Revelation of Jesus as it has been preserved in Christianity, with special regard to the Roman Catholic Church.

The Da Vinci Code, in turn, had to be rubbished, and I have seen that being very adequately done. But that in itself is not sufficient. It is the obligation of Christianity that what it has to offer be presented not just adequately but also in a way compatible with the needs of the people to whom it is addressed. This means that the Christian reply will have to answer adequately the very natural questions: 'What's in it for me?' and 'Why should I make myself accept parts of Christianity I don't like?'

Some contemporary sources whereby this presentation is made are not all that attractive. Some are simply too voluminous (such as our *Catechism of the Catholic Church*). Others, coming from professional theologians, are too intense. What I am offering here is intended to avoid these two pitfalls. I hope it will not prove to be too voluminous. And it is certainly not the work of a professional theologian.

What I am offering is in fact the results of my fortuitous 'shopping around', not unlike the Humanists. But very much unlike them, the outcome in my case was that I first came to see with strengthened conviction that in Christianity there is a promise, than which there can be no greater. More than that, within Christianity, as well as the ordinary means of achieving the fulfilment of this promise, there is even a means to verify within oneself the coming into existence of that promise. All this I wish to convey through my report of two insights about Christianity that came to me at different times in my life.

The first insight answered the question: 'What is Christianity?' The second addressed the question: 'What can I expect from my practice of Christianity?'

The first insight came to me in the Philippines in the late 1950s, in one of my earliest assignments when I had to teach a class of Fourth-Year High School students. In my preparation for class, the phrase 'to become God-along-with-God through Jesus, because of Jesus, after Jesus, and indeed, along with Jesus' occurred to me. In a shortened form I used it for my class as a useful summing-up of what Christianity really offers. This phrase is merely a variation on the text that I have referred to in the title of this book: 'Even in this world we are as He is' (1 John 4:17). In the light of that insight, some of the Bible's extreme-sounding texts, for example, 'It is no longer I who live, but it is Christ who lives in me',[1] came to mean for me something that was now not just possible for us (and not just for St Paul), but indeed verifiable.

It is true that any experience of ours of this privilege would be very far down the scale, in comparison to the experience of St Paul. But on the other hand, no matter how far down, we would still be on the same scale in the matter of being recipients of the transforming grace of God. We too, in our own way, would be 'a new creation'.[2]

The second insight did not come to me until I had been ordained for thirty years. This insight was a description of the ways that our souls can actually develop and grow. In other words, not merely is there in the Christian a likeness to Jesus, granted and increased by the Sacraments, but there is even the possibility of some personal awareness of the development of this likeness.

---

[1] Gal 2:20.
[2] 2 Cor 5:17; Col. 3:10.

Specific details of what this development is really like were given to the Catholic Church in a special and attractive form in the revelations given to St Teresa of Avila in the sixteenth century, at the time that the Protestant Reformation was gathering momentum. This resultant teaching of St Teresa reached me through the explanation and clarification given by the writings of a modern-day Carmelite nun.

Once I was introduced to these teachings, I sought out other books on this subject. These included the original works of St Teresa herself. But I must confess I preferred the more concise presentations of modern-day writers to the original works. By being offered in the situation and context of sixteenth-century Spanish contemplative nuns, the main message can be obscured, unless distilled and highlighted and then presented in contemporary language by our modern writers.

In thinking of the possibility of presenting these two insights, I knew I could not match any of the authorities I have referred to in the matter of their advanced knowledge. But then I decided that I could at least produce a summary of what St Teresa and they were saying, since I had not come across any other such summary. As well as a simplification, I was also willing to offer an outline of the step-by-step process by which I became aware of these riches of Catholic doctrine. If experiencing these graces was possible for me, it is equally possible for my reader!

Because I am not a trained theologian, I have had to depend heavily on analogies from my own experience. But I also submitted my views and summaries to a recognised theological authority, who approved of what I had to say.

So this is certainly not a full exposition compared with what the experts have to say. Yet what I have to say might still be acceptable as an advertisement, in the format of a 'testimonial from a satisfied customer'.

CHAPTER 1

THE GOOD NEWS

Now in my retirement after being a missionary priest for many years, I naturally spend time looking back over my life.

Uppermost in my mind must be my memories of being a Christian in the specific form of a missionary priest. But I really wish to write only about the mystery of my primary vocation to be a Christian, and the course of its development. This was and is the basic and most fundamental purpose of my life, no matter what format it may have taken.

The matter of our being informed of the meaning and purpose of our lives is the function and purpose of the Church that Jesus established through His Apostles. This kind of communication we call Revelation.

Revelation

If I had to use only one word to substitute for Revelation I would use the word 'a communication'.

Revelation is by its nature a communication from a source which is beyond our powers to tap into. We have to await the time when such a source decides to communicate with us. We then must accept the way in which the Revelation is made, and the contents of that Revelation.

This creation, of which we are a part, consists not just in our experience of it but also in the existence of the truths of Revelation that have been granted to us from the same source from which came our very creation and present existence. The undoubted truths of Revelation existing in themselves could be labelled 'static'. I attach this label merely to highlight the fact that the purpose of the communication we call Revelation is not just to exist but to have an effect, to bring about change. When that happens, Revelation then deserves the label 'dynamic'.

Our human nature is such that we have power to accept or reject this communication. But the communication is of such a nature that we should not do so, even if we were to find rejection not just possible but actually attractive!

First of all, the communication involved conveys to us information that there exists an interface between the infinity of God and our puny selves who are His creatures. The existence of such an interface makes possible the conveyance to us of His Good News, even if, on our side, His plans and purposes are still hidden yet still certain.

Growth of Revelation

The bottom line for each of us regarding Christianity is reached when we form our individual answer to the second of the twofold question:

1. What is the Christian Revelation that we are told we receive in our Catholic faith?

and
2. How is it happening to me?

We who are Catholics usually encounter and
absorb and are thereby changed by the Christian
Revelation when we start to get our initial understanding of our faith from our Catholic home atmosphere. Typically, this is then deepened by having our
ordinary secular education given to us in our
Catholic schools, with teaching about Christian Revelation as an essential part of the curriculum.

My memory of my first coming into conscious
contact at home with Christian Revelation happened
near Christmas time. Having heard about this God
Person, greater even than my parents, and based
somehow in the church we attended, I was puzzled
when I came in contact with several Santa Clauses in
various stores as my parents did their Christmas
shopping. Because Santa seemed to fit the bill for
God! But for me there was the further theological
difficulty that there were different Santas in different
stores. The theological discussion on the matter that
ensued between my mother and myself was short,
predictable. Certainly decisive, even if not all that
enlightening to me!

As I grew up, I had the usual Catholic education of
the time. Part of that memory is the drudgery of
memorising the answers in our catechism.

In all fairness, there is also another memory,
perhaps less vivid, but now, with hindsight, more
valued by me. Our religion lessons included Bible
history. And the selected and simplified stories of our
Bible history sections of our religious lessons really
did open my mind to possibilities for me of things
beyond the things of this world – outlines of what this
great God really is and what He has done!

Seminary training

Then, after my intermediate education, because of my vocation to the missionary priesthood, I received my additional seminary training.

Two years of philosophy were meant to teach us seminarians how to have disciplined and organised thinking so as to be able to look at how Revelation had been subjected to many questions and how answers to these questions were organised, evaluated, and presented in methodical fashion. Then four years of theology, with its various branches, which used the various disciplines of philosophy for this actual examination. Theology, based on and using the authority of Revelation and guided by it, undertook to answer questioning about the static contents of our Christian Revelation. It was always taken for granted that this was done in preparation for future tapping into its power to act as a guide in the religious aspects of our own spiritual lives and the spiritual lives of those in our pastoral care.

While philosophy expanded the area of questioning, and theology answered, expanding and going far beyond the limits of philosophy, most Christians have always had to manage with only a summary of the truths of our Catholic faith. The ensuing loyal practice of the Catholic faith showed that even the summary that most people had imbibed was yet able to make available to them the authoritative teaching of the Revelation of Jesus which was indeed to be conveyed to His followers, resulting in the spiritual fruits of their love

The Study of Theology

Practical   day-to-day   spirituality   permeated   the

atmosphere of the seminary when I was there, and formed me for living the life of a priest. But I must confess that after I started my theological studies, I found our dogma classes to be most boring. With perhaps three exceptions, the items of dogmatic and moral theology presented to us seemed merely to be adding detail to what I seemed to know already from the catechism classes of my elementary school days.

High praise for the catechism method!

I now see that the real worth of the contents of cate-chetical indoctrination did not (and indeed could not) become apparent to me until I had left the actual drudgery of memorising behind. I could then begin to make my own what was in fact originally contained in condensed form in the catechism answers that I was still carrying in my head even as I tackled my studies in theology.

High praise for the catechetical method.

But not necessarily total endorsement.

The insight that I am going on to describe came to me not through the catechetical method, and not even through my seminary studies. What I came to see so very clearly later on was of course implicit in the dogma I was taught. But it was not spelled out and highlighted for all to see unequivocally in the way it could have been.

I am hereby attempting to remedy that by highlight-ing just how good is the goodness of the Good News!

CHAPTER 2

TEACHING REVELATION

All this added seminary preparation and learning about Christianity and Catholicism culminated for me at the end of 1953 when it was completed and I was ordained a priest.

In early 1956, one of my assignments was the task of teaching Fourth-Year High School religion in our parish school in the Philippines. Now, instead of being at the receiving end of dogma, I was 'dishing it out!'

I found the change of perspective to be a startling difference. And a very challenging experience for me! And more than that, most spiritually rewarding.

With no official syllabus in operation at the time, I had first to decide on how I could best go about teaching as much Catholicism as possible within my time limits and other constraints. I concluded that in view of the incursions of Protestant sects in the area at the time, compounded by the absence of other books, I would give my students an introduction to Scripture as understood by the Catholic Church. With this in mind, I opted to start with the Gospel of Mark.

The Good News

St Mark appealed to me as suitable because not only was it the first but it was also in many ways the simplest of the Gospels. In chapter one, as early as verse fifteen, we can read the most concise summary in all the Gospels of the message of what Jesus expects of us. We read: 'Repent and believe the Good News'.[1]

When I started teaching and mentioned this text, very quickly I knew I would have to deal extensively with this initial reference to the phrase 'The Good News', because it was being constantly repeated in the rest of the Gospel.

I was of course very familiar with the phrase. I knew that St Mark was encapsulating in this phrase all that was involved first of all in the Person of Jesus, both as He was in this world and as He is in His resurrected life. For all of humankind, through Jesus, much Good News reached us in the form of information about God as Trinity, about Jesus Himself, about our subsequent relationship with God that Jesus had introduced. All of this information was the first necessary step in making accessible and available to believers the dynamic aspect of the Good News

This new level of knowledge of God, the Father of Jesus and now known as our Father too, made available to us a new motivation to love and adore this divine Father in ways which are away beyond what we human beings are capable of by ourselves. The ability to love like that was made possible for us by the loving relationship of Jesus with us. In fact, as a result of this relationship, He shares with us His priv-

[1] Mark 1:15.

ilege and even His power of honouring the Father, so
that we too can now do so in something of the way
that He Himself could and did.

All of the above, which constituted the Good News
then, was made available in the present time to us,
His followers. This was done first through the living
medium of His Apostles. Then it continued to be
done through the medium of their lawful successors.
Their influence and many teachings of theirs were
recorded in the written word by the medium of the
inspired, authorised Scriptures.

Here was the skeleton of an explanation of what
the phrase 'The Good News' is. But even a quick
outline of the skeleton has taken up numerous lines
and several paragraphs and covers many differing
aspects of our Catholicism! And I had undertaken
to teach in detail to my class the contents of these
lines!

My students had a concrete example of the Good
News of Jesus before their very eyes. It was obviously
the inspiration of this Good News which had brought
me, a young foreigner, to that somewhat remote
corner of the Philippines, to spend my life there. My
missionary priesthood and my presence in that
school in the Philippines were both living indicators
of the Good News and its being put into practice in
my case.

But living the Good News in myself was one thing.
Teaching 'the Good News' formally for the instruc-
tion, inspiration and motivation of Filipino fourth-
year students was another.

As a memory aid to my students to help them
absorb all this, I needed something far simpler than
the several lines of explanation as above. I needed a
key phrase to encapsulate it all!

Key Phrase

If I were to make this key phrase clear at the level of the understanding of the students before me, the best way to do it would be through explanatory Scripture texts, preferably from St Mark, the Gospel we were studying. Scripture texts are in themselves authoritative. I could present them for that reason and then concentrate on them, and in that way, give the students easily-remembered items from their religion classes with me, in a way which would give them a defence against the text-quoting Protestant sects that abounded there. So I urgently needed such texts.

But when I went looking through the whole Gospel of St Mark for a suitable phrase or phrases in the text to express and explain the specific contents of the Good News, no such convenient phrase presented itself to me as suitable for my purposes. St Mark freely spoke about the Good News – but never really defined it!

As in my private preparation of my lessons I wrestled with this problem, I finally realised for myself with a bit of a shock what was really on offer in the Good News. I already knew what that was, in the format of texts from different parts of the New Testament. For example there was the text from the Second Epistle of Peter: '... you will be able to share in the divine nature ...[2]' That was clear enough for me with my background of philosophy and theology. But I thought it too abstract to suit my immediate purpose, that of teaching fourth-year students who had no previous background of detailed and intensive earlier study of the catechism or of philosophy.

I wanted a text to emphasise very clearly that Jesus

---

[2] 2 Pet. 1:4

was sharing with us not just some abstract result of His Passion and Death but His whole personality! This gift to us of His sharing this Personality in fact brought with it some kind of inclusion in His actual Passion and Death and Resurrection. And therefore, inclusion in the Divine Life of the Trinity![3]

In short, He was then, and is now, sharing with us His actual and whole importance as the Son of God!

We of course could never achieve the importance by ourselves, and by our own efforts, of being the Only-Begotten Son of God. Because, seen from our perspective, this concept is for us 'the bottom line' of the Good News that Jesus was, is, and always will be, willing to share this, His very Divinity, with us.[4]

In theology, stemming especially from the writings of the Greek Fathers of the Church, this privilege, this process, is called 'divinisation'.

Other texts

However, even if Mark's writings did not offer a convenient formula that suited my needs of the

---

[3] Just recently I came across for the first time the following from Julian of Norwich who has this to say: 'And He Who out of love made man, by the same love would restore him not merely to his former bliss but to one that was even greater. <u>Just as we were made like the Trinity at our first creation,</u> so our Maker would have us like our Saviour Jesus Christ, in heaven forever by virtue of our re-creation. (My underlining.)

[4] We also have the inspiring (and challenging) words in the offertory prayers of the Mass: '... may we come to share in the divinity of Christ who humbled Himself to share in our humanity'. Also the *Catechism of the Catholic Church* quotes the Church Fathers as saying this. Para. 460.

moment, there were other texts in the New Testament which did so.

The text that first came to my attention was in the first letter of St John:

> Here and now, dear friends, we are God's children; what we shall be has not yet been disclosed, but we know that when it is disclosed, we shall be like Him because we shall see Him as He is.[5]

This was the kind of idea and phrasing that I wanted.

And when I looked farther, I found more of the same. When talking about confidence on the Day of Judgement, John writes: 'even in this world we are as He is'.[6] The directness and simplicity of the wording of these texts met my needs perfectly.

As well as meeting my needs at that time, I find this particular text so powerful that I chose it as part of the title of this book.

I now had my suitable texts as scriptural basis for the concepts that I wanted to teach.

Methodology of Teaching Revelation

To reinforce the contents of the texts, I wanted to make these insights both explicit and at the same time concise. To do so, I wanted even just one key phrase to convey to my students the immensity of what is this 'bottom line' of the Christian Revelation.

[5] John 3:2
[6] John 4:17.

For a start, there came to my mind the ponderous and complicated phrase: 'To become-God-along-with-God through Jesus, because of Jesus, after Jesus, along with Jesus'. For my teaching purposes I then shortened the phrase to the wording: 'to become God-along-with-God'.

'Adopted'

In the course of my teaching, I made sure to clarify what the Christian Revelation is, and what I was trying to convey. To do so, I also acquainted my students with the texts from St Paul[7] where we are described as 'adopted'.

Jesus is the natural and eternal Son of God. We are not. But we have been made so, to whatever extent and in whatever way and time that the love of God is offering. This is what we are told elsewhere in St Paul when he wrote:

> All of us then reflect the glory of the Lord with uncovered faces; and that same glory ... transforms us into His very likeness, in an ever greater degree of glory.[8]

And the ordinary legal term of 'adoption' is the closest example, using human-level wisdom, that St Paul could think of to suit his purposes in conveying this message.

He was conveying something that he had very

[7] Rom. 8:15–17; Gal. 4:5.
[8] 2 Cor. 3:18; translation from First Reading, week 16, Wednesday, vol. III, The Divine Office.

direct experience of, because of his special conversion process. According to himself, this special conversion turned him into a witness, and even more than a witness, an 'ambassador'[9] of Christ.

So my new phrase was an attempt to advertise for my students in an easily-remembered way all that St Paul and the total Christian Revelation was offering.

Choice, Force, Certainty

It is true that we usually do not like to be forced in any way. And if we are forced, we thereby lose the privilege of choice.

But it is equally true that we also like certainty. Uncertainty means that within us there are two or more forces in contention. So while we do not like to be forced, we also dislike uncertainty. Indeed, we sometimes crave certainty at all costs.

In our human affairs, to gain certainty, we can see little or no objection to using whatever force is at our command – physical, moral, cultural, financial, political and any other kind we can think of – for the apparently noble motive that what we do when we force is for the long-term benefit of ourselves and/or others.

In fact, our craving for certainty and for comfort might bring us to the point that we would prefer that God too would do the same. We would prefer that God would sweep us off our feet by giving us what the Mafia describe as 'an offer I cannot refuse!' – and thereby exempting us from the difficulty of the original God-given task of making our free choice. This

---

[9] 2 Cor. 5:20; Eph. 6:20.

task is in the last analysis our most highly-prized privilege of liberty! Therefore, any such arrangement whereby God would sweep us off our feet would thereby frustrate God's original and eternal plan.

So for us, it may be a mystery of the ways of God that He sees no need to do that. And if so, to this way of doing things we must conform!

Religious Development

Why couldn't I have seen all this before?

It was all there, culminating in the well-known Catholic doctrine of the Mystical Body, in which we Catholics are asked to believe.

I could now see that this doctrine of the Mystical Body was in fact a pulling together by church theologians of many scripture texts and traditions and truths. The purpose was to develop awareness of a certain aspect of our understanding of our Catholic religion. The theologians may have recognised that by being aware of many disparate items in our Catholic upbringing, we were in the position that, to some extent in matters spiritual, we 'could no longer see the wood for the trees'. Using the technical term of 'a Mystical Body', that situation was to be corrected by them by presenting us with this over-all picture.

Unfortunately, if our gaze is sometimes directed onto 'the wood', we can no longer see 'significant trees'. In this case I mean the truth described as 'divinisation'. It has always been there – but not highlighted. But 'divinisation' is the most striking description of what is possible within us as a result of our Christian Revelation. It is a key aspect – the 'bottom line' – of what our Christian Revelation really is. What is on offer in our Christian Revelation is that even now in this world we can have some awareness of the privilege and gift of God that we can 'become God-along-with-God through Jesus, because of Jesus, along with Jesus, after Jesus'.

Making the free and voluntary choice of believing in this mystery not just about Jesus alone but about the effects of Jesus in us is 'the name of the game!'

The actuality of experiencing 'divinisation' even now in the knowledge of the mystery, with its culmination in our future participation in the actual life of the Holy Trinity, is the reward for winning that game!

CHAPTER 3

THE GOOD NEWS NOW

In the introduction, I made known my intention to present two major insights into our Catholic faith that came to me over a period of years. In the last chapter, I have given the outline of what that first insight was, at the time and in the manner it came to me. As an indication of the worth I attribute to it as benefit for my spiritual life, I venture to say that in the light of this insight, my consequent heightened appreciation of this truth of our Revelation has the same value for me as the way in which a recovering alcoholic looks upon his newly-found sobriety. I look upon my present understanding of Revelation, even if belated, with the appreciation that one can have for what the psychologists describe as the 'Ah-a' experience of a revelation concerning something that we have previously taken for granted.

But more has still to be said about it before I move on to the second insight.

Feedback

Several times since I began to use the phrase 'becoming-God-along-with God', I have had feedback telling me about the shock effect on some people of such a statement. In fact, their reaction was to shy away from the phrase.

This is a pity.

I know what it is like to have such shock effect, because I experienced it myself when this phrase first came to mind! And a memory of its impact has stayed with me to this very day. But in my circumstances of having to continue to teach, I was fortunate that I had to sustain the preliminary shock effect and thereby give the phrase a fair chance for evaluation.

Shock effect

So let us take a moment to look a little more closely at 'shock effect', so as to see what exactly it is and, more importantly, to see a way through what may be the crucial obstacle preventing us from reaching the full benefits we can get from the full Christian Revelation.

When telling me about theirs, some people have implied that this kind of shock effect in religious matters is counter-productive. I remain unconvinced of this.

I counter their objections with my belief that in this day and age, all of us are in reality no strangers to shock effect. We are constantly – and inescapably – exposed to deliberately created shock effect from all the advertisements that are poured at us and over us and through us in so many different and subtle ways – all seeking our attention and many depending on unashamed shock effect to gain it!

Any new insight by its nature has to carry with it a kind of shock effect, even if so very mild as merely to the extent that something has registered with us as being new. But the stronger the shock effect, the stronger our reaction may be. And since this particular shock effect is the matter of learning something positive about the purpose of our lives, this hopefully is not going to be 'counter-productive' in its own right, unless we handle it badly!

In this day and age, the very shock effect is what may be needed to more forcefully bring the whole truth to our attention. In fact, nothing less may be sufficient! My particular expression of it is offered solely with the intention of doing precisely that. So I remain unrepentant for continuing to offer what I know can only bring about shock effect.

Non-shock effect

I recently noticed something that St Augustine had written,[1] which basically said the same thing but did not have my shock effect. In his presentation I found a clue for me to analyse where precisely and why the phrase I used had such shock effect. He wrote:

> The only-begotten died for us, that He might not remain alone, **and so the only Son of God made many[2] sons of God.** (My bold lettering)

I began to see the similarity and then the difference between what I wrote and what St Augustine wrote.

St Augustine's thought was focused on what Jesus

---

[1] Sermon 171. The Office of Readings 26 May Feast of St Philip Neri. The Divine Office vol. III.

[2] While it hardly matters, I point out that since 'many' refers to people, it might be seen as a clearer translation if it were rendered '... so the only Son of God made many **people** sons of God' (My bold lettering).

did, which of course affected us by making us sons, as he, St Augustine and St Paul before him, have said. My presentation obviously had to be based on this belief. But my presentation also had the merit that it focused starkly on the fact that it is we – I the writer and you, the reader – who have been made sons, rather than staying focused only on the Person who did so. I realise that my phrase has its shock effect precisely because I chose this particular and equally valid focus.

My deliberate isolation of the fact itself was not intended to take away anything from this truth in the way it has been expressed by St Augustine and the Catholic doctrine it expresses – each of them doing so without more than normal shock effect. On the contrary, it was and is my hope that by isolating this truth for a moment (but always keeping it in focus in relation to the truth that Jesus our Saviour has done this), I have enhanced two things. I have enhanced our awareness of what Jesus has done. I have enhanced our awareness of the potential and the opportunity that Catholicism offers to us.

In fact, when we see the shock effect, I might also claim to have thereby enhanced our awareness of the magnitude of salvation and, by its very magnitude, the desperate need we have not to neglect, minimise or even miss it in any way.

Pattern of Shock Effect

First Step

Shock effect in matters of religion (and in this case regarding my phrase) typically elicits a two-step reaction pattern.

The first reaction is: 'I am not worthy'.

It is a fact that all of us have enough evidence internally about ourselves and our shortcomings to be sufficient proof for us that we really are not worthy. So there is an unquestionable basis for this first reaction. Therefore, this reaction has undoubtedly the merit of being natural, by being true and valid, and being appropriate.

But when the whole body of Revelation is adverted to and brought into the picture, this instinctive initial reaction alone does not end the matter. This is so because it is equally true that by the very offering to us by God through Jesus of such a gift, **we have been made worthy**.

The usual word that we are accustomed to is 'salvation'. The word that St Paul uses over and over again to explain this process of salvation in us is the word: 'justified'.[3]

Second Step

And if and when that equally undoubted fact of our first instinctive reaction to shock effect is presented, and then counteracted by a deepened understanding of Revelation, the second possible step of our reaction is the very real hazard that we will then go on to say:

I do not want it!

Why should this be?
On the face of it, by the nature of what is on offer – than which there can be no greater – there should be instant and total acceptance. But on the contrary, for

[3] Rom. 3:24, 26 are the first examples of many.

our own spiritual realism, we have to recognise that there is something off-putting for us in the prospect of now having to bear the responsibility of 'becoming-God-along-with-God'. We would rather opt for the comfort of our own level. Our own comfort! Our own mediocrity! And, indeed our own independence and freedom from any and every obligation we might have to owe to another, no matter who he is!

Even God!

New Attituded and Behaviour

However, if and when we consent to absorb this shock effect and get past it, we can move on to consideration of the more practical.

In this process, there is a part that we ourselves must play to co-operate with, receive, and develop, this specifically Christian privilege. We will find it easier to do so when we are equipped and enriched with whatever knowledge we can acquire about what is possible for us. We can only get this from our Christian Catholic Revelation. If and when we do that, we can then have better and stronger convictions about what we should be doing as our response – thereby safely 'earthing' the impact of our shock effect.

CHAPTER 4

HAPPINESS VERSUS HEDONISM

The value and validity and enriching benefit of any new insight are all probably best proven by looking at whatever new attitudes and behaviour are brought into being which are consistent with and develop the contents of such an insight.

Since the validity and effectiveness of our 'becoming-God-along-with-God' starts at our baptism – in fact is the purpose, benefit and result of our receiving the sacrament of baptism – any specifically Christian attitude and behaviour should stem from that sacrament. But since we have come into existence in a community where baptism has been the order of the day for many generations, and we ourselves have never known a time when we were not baptised, the effects that baptism should have may not be so obvious simply because they are taken for granted by being so general. And these effects are not dramatic, like the descent of tongues of fire on the Apostles.[1] So it is worthwhile to ask and to review what these effects might be.

---

[1] Acts 2:3.

If we are to get a better understanding of the attitudes and behaviours appropriate to our 'becoming-
God-along-with-God' that otherwise we may take for
granted, we must take time to look at what the combination of our Christian attitudes and behaviour could
and should be, and their effects within us. For that,
we must first look at what is already there in us
before baptism and even now in the non-baptised,
and then to that add what we know should stem from
our baptism.

Self-survival

What is here within us just by our being human and
alive?

Psychologists tell us that the strongest human
instinct is that of self-preservation. We can take that
as obvious. But that is only the starting-point.

In the process of preserving ourselves, we usually
manage our affairs by making the distinction
between what is necessary and what is urgent. So
while this self-preservation is always a concern, self-
preservation does not have to be always uppermost
in our mind.

Usually, what is uppermost in our minds at any
given moment is the ever-present and all-pervasive
feeling that all the sentient creatures of God's creation
experience. This is summed up in the words: **I just
want to be happy!**

Self-survival is the ultimate necessity. But present
happiness is usually the present urgency in our lives.

Happiness – How?

All of God's creatures are going to seek and find happiness in different ways. If we take the example of the lowliest blade of grass, all that is needed for it is the presence of the conditions for survival and growth. When these conditions are fulfilled, the blade of grass is certainly described by gardeners as 'healthy'. And if any level of happiness is possible for it, then we can assume that it is 'happy'.

But for human beings, the problem is not as simple as that. Being the kind of people we are, we human beings are going to have to seek our happiness in the light of whether we include God in our consideration and management of our affairs or leave God out. We have to decide on that at some stage.

Whatever about other religious situations and understandings, for those of us who accept the Christian Revelation, and as a consequence try to be genuine Christians, we must accept and consider not just the existence of God but the existence of God-Made-Man in the Person of Jesus.

And, as I have pointed out, not just the static truth of His existence but the dynamic way in which His existence and the heritage of His teachings impinge upon our lives. The written record of our New Testament Scriptures is a medium of guidance stretching over the centuries, serving as authoritative statements of our Christian Revelation.

Traditional Authority

Our Scriptures give us countless examples of what Jesus did and also countless instructions about what our behaviour should be, so that it is specifically

Christian. But the tone of what we are told is that of a very traditional and authoritarian approach. The Scriptures seem simply to tell us:

> This is what you should do. This is what is expected of you. Do it!

This traditional authoritarian tone stems first of all from the nature of what is offered to us in Revelation. But the authoritarian tone in our Christian Revelation has been augmented and increased by being delivered to us through the medium of the Semitic setting and culture in which Jesus lived. It was still within this setting and culture that the New Testament authors wrote. Apart from traditional and cultural biases, such an authoritarian attitude was the inevitable consequence of the fact that most of the people to whom it was directed were illiterate. There really was no other way.

That is no longer the case.

Therefore, is it the solution that there should not be 'traditional authority'?

I do not think that the solution is as simple as that.

The old authority must still stand and must still be accepted. Yet we can willingly and intelligently be part of the very authority itself – but only on condition that we have a better understanding of it. So our education and its being put to proper use can assist us in still living contentedly within and under legitimate authority.

Hedonism

One aspect in our modern culture is the paramount importance given to our awareness of the presence or absence of happiness.

We must still follow our human instinct to look for happiness, as all of mankind have done. But, since it is now so prominent in people's thinking, it is thereby essential to have some Christian understanding of it, and not content ourselves with mere instinctual or cultural influences.

Happiness for Christians who combine the natural desire for happiness with acceptance of the Christian Revelation could be rightly called 'job satisfaction'.

Successful Survival

However, once we even think of that, and once we go looking for authoritative information and knowledge about happiness, especially religious happiness, we can find some specific references to happiness in our Scriptures.

Apart from texts which I have already cited earlier in this book, we could add the following: 'Now that you know this, happiness will be yours if you behave accordingly' (John 13:7). 'I am going now to prepare a place for you, and after I have gone and prepared you a place, I shall return to take you with Me' (John 13:2). 'My Father will love him and we shall come to him and make our home with him' (John 14:23). 'The knowledge that I have now is imperfect; but then I shall know as fully as I am known' (1 Corinthians 13:2).

Such texts may have been adequate and sufficient

in the previous situation of the majority of Christians being illiterate and uneducated. We still need their basic contents. But we can – and indeed, must – process the contents further in accordance with our educational abilities if we are to gain from them the potential they have for helping us present-day Christians who have to live in a hedonistic world.

Speculation

One of the 'perks' of our formal education is the ability to imagine and to speculate. This God-given ability can be put to good use by us to bridge the gap between what we know for certain in Scripture, and what we need to know about happiness. Knowing what we are doing, we can venture to go ahead and speculate further about what are the effects of our Christian Revelation received by us in baptism in the matter uppermost in our minds; that of happiness.

When I have attempted this for myself, I have found the results to be an encouragement.

We are, of course, limited in what we are about to do. It is as if our artistic materials for making a picture of something which is in itself colourful are limited to black and white. This is true because we are speculating about eternity and infinity, and to do so, we are limited to our own present finite and temporal experience.

Our Experience in the Womb

As an example of the magnitude of this task, we could imagine ourselves as being back in our mother's womb, wondering what the future may hold for us. If that were to have happened, all we could have done would be to think of what we have already experienced in the womb and project that into the future.

Obviously, as we very well know now from our actual experience, there is much more available to us outside the womb than what is available to us while we were still there. Yet, whatever we have experienced will not be terminated or negatived, but expanded, even if that expansion will take us beyond our ability to imagine at that stage. Our little experiences will be still valid.

With this *caveat,* we can now acquire from our own imaginative abilities, guided by Scripture, some knowledge of what could be a description of what will be possible.

What is possible is a heightened awareness of the appropriate attitude towards happiness that we should now have as we try to fulfil the conditions laid down by Jesus. These are the conditions consistent with our present process of and preparation for our 'becoming God-along-with God', with its on-going and increasing happiness. Therefore, in following my natural instinct, and still wanting to be happy right now, I also recognise that:

By Revelation, and by no other means, God has promised that there awaits me a happiness more intense and more permanent than anything I can experience or even imagine in the here-and-now.

This happiness is of a different, higher order than anything I have yet experienced:

This happiness will be able to satisfy me perfectly and completely, which no present happiness can ever do:

This happiness is beyond my power to achieve, but is possible as God's gift to me from His love:

This complete, eternal new happiness is something that God is able to give not just to me but to all His elect:

This communion with the rest of God's creation in their happiness will bring with it even to me its special joy, without anything like competition, aggression, envy, jealousy of other who will like-wise be benefited.

A pre-requisite for achieving and enhancing the 'job satisfaction' capacity within us Christians concerning our religion is our understanding of what our human condition really is. When we have these basics in place, by making them our own, we are in a better position to augment the response to God's Revelation that we are already making.

CHAPTER 5

REPENT – GENERAL

In chapter two I quoted the summary in St Mark's Gospel of what Jesus expects from us, His followers, namely the words: 'Repent and believe the Good News.'[1] There are two parts to this summary. In chapters 3 and 4, I looked at the second part: 'Believe the Good News.' Now we must look at the first part: 'Repent'.

These two parts, which differ in what they put before us are still the polarities of what is one single message – two sides of the one coin. Taking one polarity on its own and fulfilling it exclusively is not enough. Both directives are needed. So both directives need individual, careful examination. Then they must be re-combined in our thinking and this thinking used to guide us in acting according to the unified message they have put before us.

But such re-combining is not all that simple. Along with our privilege of accepting the Good News and living in accordance with it, we are in the hazardous position of being able to ignore or contradict all that we are told in the Good News.

[1] Mark 1:15.

Free Will – Positive and Negative

The points I made about genuine God-given happiness in the last chapter are the fleshing out of what the potential for our happiness through the Good News is going to mean for us in the future. While we rejoice in this knowledge, we must also recognise that as rational beings, we know that we must act even now in accordance with this blueprint for a happiness of which we can catch a glimpse right now but the completion and reality of which will be eternal and infinite.

All of which is more easily said than done. Because we must recognise that as rational beings, we have a mixture of power, privilege and obligation to accept this system of God's.

We do have free will, for our management of this most potent of mixtures.

But by having free will, we also experience the hazard that we can refuse to manage our affairs as we ought to.

It is true that we have a safe-guard, our conscience, to guide us. But we also know how easy it is to override this conscience.

Having a free will is like having a mental gear-shift. We are familiar with the gear levers in our cars. Most of their various positions are arranged so as to take us forward at differing speeds. But there is also one that takes us backwards! Just as a driver of a car must know the gears if he is to be successful in his driving, and avoid disaster, we need to know our mental gears which are our means of access to our spiritual gears!

I propose that we first review the one that has the potential to take us backwards in spiritual matters, and therefore, not in the direction we want to go.

External Influence

There are two influences pushing us in this direction, one external, one internal. In Genesis we are told of the existence of this external influence. The Genesis story starts with Creation and then the Fall of mankind. But if we are to organise our knowledge into a strictly logical pattern, we should see the beginnings of our history as including the fact of the existence prior to ours of a Malevolent Being.

In the Genesis story, in accordance with the *genre* of that presentation, the Malevolent Being is presented as the serpent.[2] The influence of this Malevolent Being had a crucial bearing on the decision taken by our First Parents,[3] and therefore on the fate of all mankind, up until now, and therefore including ourselves.

We do not have as much detailed information about this Being as we might like. But in Revelations, we read about the Great Dragon, 'the primeval serpent, known as the devil or Satan ...'.[4]

Existance and Influence

We have no reason to doubt the continuing existence and influence of this powerful Being. All around us in the present and in the past, there are countless examples of evil. In view of mankind's most basic instinct towards self-survival, evils are not the genuine desires of mankind, even though

---

[2] Gen. 3:1.
[3] *Catechism of the Catholic Church*, pp. 78–94.
[4] Rev. 12:9.

many evils can be attributed to mankind's behaviour. Certainly the most plausible explanation is the existence not just of God but the existence of the Malevolent Being referred to in Genesis. We have this confirmed in the Gospels when we are told of three levels of temptation that this Malevolent Being used against Jesus.[5]

Jesus considered this Being to be very real and very powerful, warning Peter ahead of time about a temporary victory by this Being over him:

> Simon, Simon! Satan, you must know, has got his wish to sift you all like wheat; but I have prayed for you, Simon, that your faith may not fail, and once you have recovered, you in your turn must strengthen your brothers.'[6]

Satan Now

But outside the Catholic Church the reality of Satan has nowadays been treated in two different ways. Strangely, one is the contradiction of the other!

In the one which is most common, more pervasive and perhaps more attractive, this major concept of the existence of Satan or the Devil has been discarded by many as unpalatable, incredible, medieval, etc. People now simply deny belief in the existence of such a Being.

The implication for us Christians is that many of us must live out our Christianity in an atmosphere which derides belief in this crucial truth, so that we

---

[5] Matt. 4:1–10.
[6] Luke. 22:31–32.

must first hold on to our firm conviction of the existence of this Malevolent Being. After that, we need our informed faith to assure us that the power of the Devil is never anything beyond the power of God to control.

Satanism

In the second, contradictory aberration, a small number of people have seen that the Devil's temptations can be of such a kind and of such magnitude that, when successful, they have consequences for the whole of the human race. In the absence of the security of our Catholic faith, some people have then gone to the extent of taking two steps contrary to that faith. They first believe that the Devil is nowadays proving himself to be more powerful than God. And the second step is that they consider it a smart move to join this 'winning' force. This is Satanism.

We Catholics must now spend our lives in circumstances where we are liable to be influenced by either or both of these untruths. However, we know we can depend on the wisdom and authority of the Catholic Church so that we can receive this power of God for our protection. When this is true, we can continue our lives in a stance and belief in the truths about Satan which lie between these two extremes.

Internal Influence: Temptations

While it is true that temptations can come to us directly from the Evil One, as happened to Jesus (and we must therefore attribute certain kinds of temptation to the influence of this Being), it is also true that temptations can come to us from our very selves. So it is not merely useful but downright essential for many of us to have at our fingertips the authoritative information we have from St Paul about the effects of both kinds of temptations.

Consequences Affecting Creation

We start with what St Paul had to say about the effect on Creation itself of this diabolical reality. We are given such a description in the following:

> For I reckon that the sufferings we now endure bear no comparison with the splendour, as yet unrevealed, which is in store for us. For the created universe waits with eager expectation for God's sons to be revealed. It was made the victim of frustration, not by its own choice, but because of him who made it so; yet always there was hope, because the universe itself is to be freed from the shackles of mortality and enter upon the liberty and splendour of the sons of God. Up to the present, we know, the whole created universe groans in all its parts as if in the pangs of childbirth. Not only so, but even we, to whom the Spirit is given as firstfruits of the harvest to come, are groaning inwardly, while we wait for God to make us His sons and set our whole body free.[7]

---

[7] Rom. 8:18–23.

Consequences affecting Individuals

The consequences of Original Sin are so all-pervasive that even St Paul, with all his privileges, cannot avoid them but must still experience them. In his letter to the Romans he writes:

> The Law, of course, is spiritual, but I am unspiritual; I have been sold as a slave to sin. I cannot understand my own behaviour. I fail to carry out the things I want to do, and I find myself doing the very things I hate. When I act against my own will, that means that I have a self that acknowledges that the Law is good, and so the thing behaving in that way is not myself but sin living in me. The fact is, I know of nothing good living in me – living, that is, in my unspiritual self – for though the will to do what is good is in me, the performance is not, with the result that instead of doing the good things I want to do, I carry out the sinful things I do not want. When I act against my will, then, it is not my true self doing it, but sin which lives in me.
>
> In fact, this seems to be the rule, that every single time I want to do good, it is something evil that comes to hand. In my inmost self I dearly love God's Law, but I can see that my body follows a different law which battles against the law that my reason dictates. This is what makes me a prisoner of that law of sin which lives inside my body.
>
> What a wretched man I am! Who will rescue me from this body doomed to death? Thanks be to God, through Jesus Christ our Lord![8]

[8] Rom. 7:14–25.

What St Paul had to say here applied first of all to a specific difficulty that he and all the other Jewish Christians had to face. This is the tension between the very genuine Old Covenant, consented to and adhered to by Jesus Himself, and the New Covenant instituted by His Death and Resurrection. While there was a chain of continuity, this quantum leap by the very magnitude of the expansion of the possibilities offered constituted an element of a break.

When the early Christian converts within Judaism had to make the choice of accepting the New Covenant instituted by Him, Jesus Himself was not with them in person in the same visible, tangible way He had been to the Apostles. When these converts did make the choice and became Christians, they were, from their point of view, having to go beyond the Mosaic Law current at the time, so as to complete it.[9] But in the minds of the Jewish authorities, they were thereby in many ways going against the Law which was the backbone of the Old Covenant.

In our present-day Catholic situation, that element of forced choice in this particular matter has disappeared over the course of the centuries. However, we in turn have to face different choices with different degrees of difficulty. The tensions that St Paul so unequivocally experienced in himself are still applicable to the less intense situations in which the majority of us pass our Christian lives.

---

[9] Matt. 5:17.

CHAPTER 6

REPENT – CATHOLIC CHURCH TEACHING

To have a better understanding of some aspects of present-day Catholic Church teaching, it may help if we have a preliminary look at the source of that teaching.

The Catholic Church was established within the parameters that Jesus accepted for Himself. Jesus was a Jew. He taught exclusively within the boundaries of that nation. The entire membership of the church He founded were Jewish. It is only natural that our Scriptures should be coloured by the style of thinking and speaking which was typical of the Jewish people, and indeed of Jesus Himself, as we see it in the Gospels.

It is therefore not just useful but actually very necessary that we can recognise and identify this particular style, and then make appropriate allowance for it. So one could say that the present Catholic Church still speaks with a Jewish accent. It is therefore worthwhile to look at what that Jewish accent might be.

Semitic Thinking

The description 'Semitic' comes from the application
of the name of the eldest son of Noah[1] ('Sem' in older
translations, now 'Shem' in the Jerusalem Bible
version), to classify peoples of the Middle East in a
way which included the Jews or Israelites.

The main characteristic Semitic thinking is the very
great dependence on the 'high-voltage' form of
presentation by the exclusive use of only two possibilities, namely, 'all' or 'nothing'. This characteristic
of Semitic style of thinking can be described as
'binary', limiting our considerations to only two
possibilities of 'all' or 'nothing'. (This is the basis of
the working of our modern-day computers.) In the
absence of finer distinctions between them, each
possibility cannot avoid seeming to be given something of an extreme nature.

An example of this kind of thinking in English is:
'I'll be there and back in no time at all!'

Perhaps the best-known example of this kind of
thinking in the New Testament is in the text: 'You
must love the Lord your God with all your hear, with
all your soul and with all your mind ... You must
love your neighbour as yourself'.[2]

The most extreme example in the New Testament
may well be in Matthew 25:29: ... but from the man
who has not, even what he has will be taken away.[3]

---

[1] Gen. 10:1, 32.
[2] Matt. 22:37, 39.
[3] Matt. 25:29.

Paradox

At this point, it may be useful to make a distinction. Early in the Gospel of Matthew,[4] we find that not merely has it its usual Semitic thinking, but also it is even couched in paradox. This is the Beatitudes section of the Sermon on the Mount, with each section starting with the word 'Happy' even though the statements there are not conducive to happiness as we understand it.

The biblical scholars tell us that that Matthew was writing for Jewish Christians who were suffering the injustice of being expelled from the synagogues, and for all intents and purposes thereby expelled from the Jewish nation. So Matthew, as it were, was both expressing the depths of their misery but then adding the message of hope that the Good News of Jesus can bring even to the most extreme of circumstances.

Greek Thinking

What may somewhat obscure the meaning for us of these Semitic texts is the fact that we are accustomed to a different model of thinking. We are accustomed to a Greek-thinking model, and unconsciously use it in our everyday way of speaking. The characteristic we are interested in here is labelled 'analogue'. This means that we are given divisions and options on a scale which runs between the 'all' and the 'nothing' that Semitic thinking limits itself to. (Clocks which show all the figures between one and twelve are classified with this label).

[4] Matt. 5:1–12.

Semitic Thinking about Sin

If we are aware of the way of thinking of St Paul and the Semitic style of his writings, what his message actually is can be made clearer for us. This is very obvious in the presentations of his description in the last chapter of the sinful tendencies that he saw within himself and us. In chapter seven of Romans, we read in verse seventeen: 'It is no longer I who perform the action but sin that lodges in me.'

After outlining the problem so dramatically, St Paul then gives the solution, or antidote. This is indicated in the final verse of that particular section: 'Who is there to rescue me out of this body doomed to death? God alone, through Jesus Christ our Lord! Thanks be to God!'[5]

We can think of Semitic thinking as floating over all possible implications in this kind of statement, because Semitic thinking, as it were, rushes on to get immediately to the main point. In this case the main point is the antidote to all the tensions that Paul has been talking about.

As he described these tensions in himself, he was thereby describing the tensions in turn in each of us, when we have to make the choice between what is attractive but sinful, and what is right, yet often unattractive.

Catholic Church Teaching

However, while the essentials of the Semitic presentations are enduringly true, their message has been preserved, developed and interpreted for us in the teachings of the Catholic Church.

[5] Rom. 7:24–5.

With the source of the message so uncompromis-
ingly absolute in its Semitic thinking, and the people
for whom it is intended today being people who are
more comfortable with the 'analogue' or Greek way
of thinking, we very much need the combination of
authority and wisdom of the Catholic Church. The
Church is called upon to manage the transition
whereby the 'voltage' of the message has been
stepped down from its Semitic intensity of Genesis
and St Paul into presentations more congenial to our
modes of thinking and speaking.

This 'stepping-down' of the intensity of the message
took time. For our purposes at this point, we can look
at one such adaptation which came into being during
the fifth century. That was when St Augustine had to
engage in controversy with a man called Pelagius.
Perhaps in sincere efforts to encourage people to exert
more effort in responding to the call of Jesus, Pelagius
went too far in his efforts to 'step-down' the 'voltage'
of Genesis. Without perhaps intending to do so, he
minimised the effects of the sin of Adam and Eve. He
did so by giving a key role to human effort alone. In
this controversy, St Augustine found it useful to coin
the phrase 'Original Sin'. And this label has been used
by the Catholic Church ever since.

In its Easter Saturday Vigil liturgy the Church has
traditionally used the phrase: '*O felix culpa!* O happy
fault'. Spiritual writers such as Julian of Norwich[6]

---

[6] 'And He Who out of love made man, by the same love
would restore him not merely to his former bliss but to one
that was even greater. Just as we were made like the Trinity
at our first creation, so our Maker would have us like our
Savour Jesus Christ, in heaven forever by virtue of our re-
creation'. *Revelations of Divine Love*, Clifton Wolters (tr.),
Penguin Classics, ch. 10, p. 78.

have elaborated upon this apparent contradiction in our Revelation that Original Sin could be labelled 'a happy fault'!

Vatican II has confirmed and elaborated on the doctrine always held by the Catholic Church, when the Council refers to symptoms of a deeper dichotomy that is in man himself. Vatican II[7] has this to say:

> man ... became out of harmony with himself, with others, and with all created things. Therefore man is split within himself. As a result, all of human life, whether individual or collective, shows itself to be a dramatic struggle between good and evil, between light and darkness. Indeed, man finds that by himself he is incapable of battling the assaults of evil successfully , so that everyone feels as though he is bound with chains.

This statement is a fleshing-out of the well-known quotation from St Augustine in his autobiography: 'O Lord ... you have made us for Yourself and our hearts find no rest until they rest in You.'

Repentance for Actual Sin

We all like to hear the statement in Genesis that we have been made 'in the likeness of God'.[8] And we all have a sense of being fundamentally well-intentioned

---

[7] See *Gaudium et Spes* (Pastoral Constitution on The Church in the Modern World), Ch. I sections 12–14, with this quotation taken from section 13.
[8] Gen. 1:27.

persons, at the very least. So any suggestion of anything wrong or flawed or 'sin' in us seems at first sight to be a contradiction.

In the light of that instinctive feeling, at first glance the word 'repent', if applied to us, can seem almost unnecessary. We will certainly agree that theoretically, it could apply to us, since we are all capable of falling into serious sin. But we take it for granted that for the usual repentance of what we know to be sins, we have first of all the mechanism of our consciences to give us the conviction to repent. We also accept that we need the grace of God to help us to follow through on this conviction.

But we feel we are already using this grace. After all, in the Catholic Church, we have the sacramental power in a special way in the Sacrament of Reconciliation to confirm to us that this repentance has happened and is effective. Therefore, because of all our good intentions, we will already be repenting of any sins our conscience accuses us of.

Extent of Repentance

All this means that if we do not have a sense of having committed serious sins in the past or feel guilty of them now, we might be inclined to overlook the significance of this command of the Lord that we should repent.

But the demand on us of the concept 'Repent' is more than just that! The demand is that we consciously undertake to remove all that separates us from the perfection that goes with our 'becoming-God-along-with-God' which we will need so as to enter fully into the life of the Trinity. After all, Jesus has said: 'You must therefore be perfect just as your Heavenly Father is perfect'.[9]

If what separates us is sin (even the most serious), that is where we start. But if we do not have this kind of serious sin (and I imagine that most readers of this type of book are free from serious sin), we must still start to 'Repent' at whatever stage we are.

Naturally, as we progress in the spiritual life, the matters about which we repent can get smaller and smaller in terms of objective gravity.

To illustrate this, I take the historical detail that when the threat of the dissolution of the Jesuits was seen as a possibility, St Ignatius was once asked how he would manage in such an event. He replied that he thought it would take him twenty minutes to be reconciled to God's Will in this regard I then point out that if in the plan of God he should have been able to be reconciled in ten minutes, and not in twenty, then St Ignatius would have needed to have repented of his hypothetical tardiness of ten minutes!

Alcoholics Anonymous

After having looked at the hypothetical example of St Ignatius, we could come closer to experience which is available to us just by looking at the system of Alcoholics Anonymous (AA).

This system seems to me to give us not just information on the step-by-step process of repenting from a specific drug abuse, alcohol, starting even from the depths of helplessness, hopelessness and despair, but indicates how far this blessed repen-

[9] Matt. 5:48.

tance can bring us. And I believe that the whole system brings us to a point at which those who benefit from the system are putting into practice what it is that the virtue we call Christian charity would call on us to do in all circumstances, and not just in the special circumstances of the abuse of alcohol.

The system specifically limits itself to the management of alcohol abuse. But the wisdom underpinning the system is such that it has been applied to many other problems. I have even seen the figure of one hundred other systems offered in this matter.

Our interest is of course that perhaps we can bring to our consideration of Christian repentance the human wisdom in this system. And here I can cite the word 'transition' and apply it to the change that the AA system can bring about. In a previous abuser of alcohol the AA system can make him into a channel of grace to save others who are still abusing that drug. It is a concrete application of the words of St Paul:

> He (God) comforts us in all our troubles, so that we in turn may be able to comfort others in any trouble of theirs and to share with them the consolation we ourselves receive from God.[10]

So from this concrete, human-level example, we can extrapolate to our Christian repentance. It is not just a 'freedom from' when we free ourselves from the bonds and the guilt of sin. It can and should reach as far as being a 'freedom to', when, no longer

[10] 2 Cor. 1:4.

shackled by our own bonds of sin, we can then in turn be an influence on others.

AA supplies the human-level underpinnings necessary for what Jesus said to be put into practice by us:

> You are light for the world. A city built on a hill-top cannot be hidden. No-one lights a lamp to put under a tub; they put it on the lamp-stand where it shines for everyone in the house. In the same way, your light must shine in people's sight, so that, seeing your good works, they may give praise to your Father in heaven.[11]

But we Christians may add our specifically Christian dimension by adding our specifically Christian intention in using that human-level system.

Extreme Case

As well as that, our correct understanding of Christian repentance will enable us to think of its application even to the sin of Judas.

The Church has always refused to declare that Judas is in Hell because the Church has no way of knowing whether or not there was genuine repentance in the heart and soul of Judas during his last moments. Repentance therefore has such power and importance that it could have been enough to save even him from Hell.

Repentance then, understood as above, has application at every level, reaching all the way from the

---

[11] Matt. 5:14–16 (The Jerusalem Bible).

hypothetical example I have given, all with the purpose of preparing and inspiring us to reach new heights in our spiritual lives.

CHAPTER 7

REPENT NOW

It suffices for my purposes that in the previous chapter, I took a cursory look at some authoritative statements about Original Sin, starting with a reference to the original sources in Scripture and jumping to the recent teaching of Vatican II and the *Catechism of the Catholic Church*. Even in these skimpy references we can see the same revealed truth being preserved and handed on. We might also note in these authoritative statements the 'stepped-down voltage' of the manner of presentation.

Disbelief

Nowadays, the Catholic Church is faced with disbelief among many in the world. They refuse to believe that there is a Malevolent Being in existence. Then they refuse to believe that there is such a thing as sin. Many others, who may or may not believe in its existence, do not want sin to be discussed and would resent discussion of guilt and sin and accountability before God some time in the future. They would thereby deny the remit and the authority of the

Catholic Church to discuss it, labelling it as undue interference with the liberty of others.

They consider that such discussion is on the wrong track, because they believe that they can adequately explain away the signs and symptoms of Original Sin such as Catholics see, as 'merely a developmental flaw, a psychological weakness, a mistake, or the necessary consequence of an inadequate social structure etc'.[1]

Sin as Action

Our usual use of the words 'sin' and 'imperfections' in the Catholic Church applies to deliberate actions of one kind or another, even the 'action' of omitting something we should do. And equally in the Catholic Church, we believe that the possibility of sin, until we are united with God, is always a real hazard in our spiritual lives. And if and when the hazard happens, we then have the second-level hazard: *Will I repent? When? How?* But the Catholic Church has wisdom and guidance and God-given authority in responding to these questions.

The Church sees the hazard in life of committing actual sin as the kind of hazard that sailors experience and have to manage when they can see rocks sticking out of the water. In cases like that, the hazard is obvious. The solution is equally obvious: 'Avoid the hazard! Or, if not avoided, repent of it as soon as possible!'

---

[1] *'The Catechism of the Catholic Church'*, p. 87, para. 387.

Sin as State

There is another kind of hazard which also needs repentance. This is the hidden hazard not just of actions or of omissions. It is the real hazard of our being in a 'state',[2] into which we are born. This is the hazard of Original Sin.

While such a concept is rejected out-of-hand by so many, and is an uncomfortable truth for those of us who believe, Original Sin is the reality with which we have to live. The situation can be likened to the hazard for sailors of rocks just under the surface of the water. Such a hazard is manageable, just as the hazard of hidden reefs can be managed by sailors who have accurate maps. But we have been well warned by Pope Paul VI that the world has lost its sense of sin. The world, in general has thrown away the map!

In short, we may find ourselves demanding 'a level playing pitch' for our religious endeavours. God has given us one with bumps and potholes!

The Modern Challenge

As a result, nowadays, the Catholic Church is faced with a kind of controversy different from that of previous centuries. Instead of arguing about what Original Sin consists of, and how it affects us, as in the time of Pelagius and St Augustine, and even up until the religious controversies of the sixteenth century, we are faced with the kind of controversy that stems from disbelief among many in the world

[2] Ibid.

that there is such a thing as sin, either actual or Original.

All this is in spite not just of the message of Revelation but even of all the evidence around us and within us!

It is of course most consoling to know the final glorious outcome, as contained in the Good News, and to know that in baptism we have received entry into that process. But, pending its coming to pass, could we find out more, even if only about how Original Sin starts in us and how it grows?

So, depending on the certain truths of the previous chapter as our foundation and anchor, we may be able to go on to another 'step-down' in the 'voltage' of our considerations of 'Repent' and 'Original Sin'.

'Centre of the Universe' – Physical

When we look at the application of these truths in our own case and in our very own experience, our first reaction is automatically on the feeling level.

We all have our awareness of ourselves as the starting-point of our feelings. And we all have a sense of being fundamentally well-intentioned persons, at the very least. Indeed, we have the statement in Genesis that we have been made 'in the likeness of God'.[3] But this very 'likeness of God' that we are so glad to hear about can be exercised in a way which is summed up in the statement – a partial truth indeed but still the truth – that **'I am the Centre of the Universe!'**

Yes! When we hear this phrase, our first reaction may be to think that it is exaggerated. But it is not. It

[3] Gen. 1:27.

certainly is limited. But it is not exaggerated.

Just think of it for a moment. Where I am standing or sitting at present, part of the universe is in front of me, another part is behind me. More of it is above me, and more again is below me. And the same is true as regards any direction starting from any side of me that I can name. So this statement is certainly true, physically and geographically.

'Centre of the Universe' – Psychological

We may not have consciously adverted to it, but the statement '**I am the Centre of the Universe**' characterises all my experience after I am born – and even for some time before that, when in our development in the womb we have reached the point of being self-aware!

The universe of which I am the centre can be very small at first. It can be no more than the expanse of my mother's arms and her caring for me. But my perception of this universe expands. As it expands, my tiny hands reach out to grasp whatever is there, no matter what it is. I bring it to my mouth to experience and even, if possible, to absorb it.

When in my mother's arms I cried. And when I did, good things happened. Here was my first taste of power: 'I can cause things to happen!' Not very many things, even though I slowly increase the number as I develop skills. But they are all of greatest importance to me.

Shortly after that, I come in contact with the saddening reality that I have not just desires and expectations but also very definite limitations.

Yet, even so, a time will come when we reach the point of being able to know about the many wonders in this world and even about the wonders of outer space. But while all this is happening, there is no suggestion that the original previous tendencies about my central importance have been eliminated. I am always the centre of all that exists! (With the proviso of course: 'As far as I am concerned!')

Management – Positive

We can learn to manage this situation in one of two ways. The first way is that we can learn to manage it under the influence of and in accordance with a belief in God.

Even though Genesis uses only figurative language, such figurative language can still convey a message of encouragement. It is true that one tree was the source of our downfall, by having been used badly by our First Parents.[4] It is true that we are told of the tough conditions under which we – and I – must now survive. But in the imagery put forward in Genesis,[5] we are specifically told that nothing happened to the second tree, the Tree of Life.[6] And this can be a symbol of hope for us humans in our exile. I, the Centre of the Universe, can still aspire to reach that tree!

Management – Negative

But we humans can also attempt to manage our affairs in the second way which is by rejecting God.

---

[4] Gen. 3:1–7.
[5] Gen. 3:16–19, 23–24.
[6] Gen. 3:22.

For those of us who have not done so, it may be difficult to imagine it. But since this rejection of God has been done so blatantly in the last few centuries, scholars have had a chance to study the phenomenon. They have said:

> In rejecting God, we have not rejected the functions properly attributed to God, but merely taken them as our own. It is now we who define good and evil; we who define birth, life and death; and we who shall create ourselves according to the image we happen to desire.[7]

Here is the travesty of the genuine Good News. Here is the extreme form of the hazard that we are specifically warned about:

> The Church ... knows very well that we cannot tamper with the revelation of original sin without undermining the mystery of Christ.[8]

Happiness

But whether we believe in God or not, there is something common to both of these positions. This is our instinctive seeking for happiness. This universal tendency towards happiness was mentioned in our description of the Good News and outlined in view of our awareness of the contents of the Good News.

So, in our human condition, we are in fact

---

[7] Donald de Marco and Benjamin Wiker, '*Architects of the Culture of Death*', Ignatius Press, Introduction, p. 18.

[8] *Catechism of the Catholic Church*, p. 87, para. 389.

inescapably faced with a choice between two kinds of pressure and tension.

Even when we go along with God's plan for us there is pressure from this state of Original Sin.

But if we are seduced by the idea that we can avoid that pressure by the simple expedient of avoiding God, we will still find that we are faced only with a different pressure, that of tackling the difficulty of trying to fill by ourselves the vacuum created by not believing in God.

Happiness of the Infant

In either of these situations, how can we strive for happiness?

We can speculate that the following are valid statements about what goes on in an infant's awareness.

Since I start my life with no prior knowledge of Revelation, I therefore depend on my natural basic reactions of 'like' and 'dislike'. So my knowledge of happiness must then be confined only to what I have actually experienced.

Any happiness we can experience can go no further than what we are capable of experiencing at that time.

Yet we quickly learn that no happiness we can experience is fully and completely satisfying for long.

Any greater happiness (if such there be) must therefore be achieved solely by our own efforts.

If others are looking for the same as us, they can be a threat to our success in achieving it.

There will be a special joy for us in having something that no-one else has, or can acquire.

Maturation

Obviously people in every culture develop and mature, so that no matter whether they believe in God or not, they do not remain completely in this infantile frame of mind all their lives. So, in different cultures, management of this desire for happiness must come about at the humanistic level that is of course possible and indeed very often laudable. But in the absence of belief in God and in Revelation, there is no convincing motivation for going much beyond these infantile tendencies.

But when we take the Good News into consideration and have come to some awareness of it, we now have a motivation – and indeed an urgency – that these tendencies still remaining must be managed in a specifically Christian manner. A humanistic level, no matter how noble, is not sufficient.

So the reception of the Good News does not totally dispel the tension involved in seeking happiness. In baptism, we do receive our introduction to and inclusion in Christian Revelation and its Good News. But we receive this grace while still experiencing the effects of Original Sin. So, even after receiving our induction into our participation in the Good News, we are still prone to the tendencies that can impel us to dispense with the necessity of giving God His rightful place in our lives.

Transition

That means that we have a need of a transition from these, our initial tendencies in seeking happiness, to newly-acquired tendencies in the light of the information we have received from the Good News. Without going deeper into discussion on the nature of Original Sin, we can still highlight something of its effects by putting together for comparison the two differing sets of tendencies that we find within ourselves, first of all just by being human, but then being human beings who have found ourselves called to the implications and the standards of the Good News of Jesus Christ. We can assemble and compare the different tendencies, so that we can see more clearly some outline of the Christian tension that is unavoidable.

Obviously, the outline I have given opposite is not a theological statement about Original Sin. It is no more than some psychological symptoms. The symptoms of a disease are not the germs that cause it. But the symptoms are what doctors make use of to direct them to the germs. In the same way, acceptance of the existence in ourselves of these tendencies could be a help in making the theology of Original Sin more real for us.

I just want to be happy

Natural Instinct	Transition	Good News Motivation
Right Now. (It's no good if it's not right now!)		I am willing to wait because what I'm waiting for will be better, and worth waiting for.
By getting more and more of what I have already experienced.		Then get more and more of what I have not yet experienced.
Sufficient to satisfy me completely, here and now (I think).		Sufficient to satisfy me completely, even if still in the far-off future.
Which I can acquire by myself.		Which will come to me as God's gift.
Even if others have to get hurt in the process (because they too want the same as I do, and want it their way!)		Not just to me, but in future union with all who accept and follow God's way.

CHAPTER 8

THE TRANSITION PROCESS

From the beginning of my writing this book, it has been my intention to share with others the slowly-dawning appreciation of our Catholic faith that I have been privileged to come to during the course of my life.

This is an appreciation first of all of the sheer magnitude of what is actually possible. Secondly, it is an appreciation of the existence of detailed knowledge of the developmental process that is possible for us in and through our Christianity, our Catholicism.

The Two Magnitudes

Very likely, people who have read the previous chapters describing these two magnitudes will have had the same reaction as I always have when I think of them. After reading about the possibility of 'becoming-God-along-with-God', I find myself saying: 'I am not as good as that!' And after reading about sin, I then say: 'I am not as bad as that!'

Nevertheless, these two magnitudes are the 'raw

material' of the spiritual life that is possible for
human beings like ourselves.

These two apparently contradictory magnitudes,
existing in some way in us at the same time, hold us
in a tension that must be managed by ourselves. We
thereby find ourselves to be practically spiritual
'Siamese twins'.

Even for Siamese twins, there can be a successful
surgical intervention. So with us. The dynamic
element in our spiritual life is that we do not have to
stay that way! There has been the intervention of
Jesus. Our task as Christians is to make that intervention our own!

The Third Magnitude

I have presented what may seem to be the extremes
contained in our Christian, Catholic faith as preparation for presenting the wonder, and therefore the
magnitude also, of the transition that is possible for
us This third magnitude is the magnitude of what
takes place in us if and when we are really to be trans-
formed from the extreme of Original Sin to the
extreme of our deserving the title 'an altogether new
creature'.[1]

The first two magnitudes are of their nature static.
But the third magnitude is very clearly dynamic,
since, even if depending on our own volition, it is
going to be allowed to happen in us.

---

[1] Gal. 6:15. See also: Eph. 4:13; Col. 3:9; 1 Thess. 4:2; 2 Thess.
2:14.

Transition – What

Let me assemble the bits and pieces of information that are available to us in our Revelation concerning this transition. These bits and pieces come to us in various concepts.

In our Scripture we have been given a vocabulary describing concepts with which we are familiar, concepts ranging from hell to heaven. On the negative side we have 'damnation', 'condemnation', 'enmity with God', 'guilt'. On the positive side we have 'contrition', 'repentance', 'mercy', 'forgiveness', 'salvation', 'redemption', 'justification', 'sanctification'.

Each applies to the spiritual life, but applies with a special emphasis on one aspect of the whole purpose of our lives as rational, volitional human beings.

But each, by its nature, is somewhat static!

Yet there is also in the Good News dynamic concepts such as the ideas of 'hope', 'change', 'improvement', 'advancement', 'development', and 'growth', all contributing in some way to the over-arching concept not just of God's love for us but also contributing to the concept and understanding of our love for God.

Transition

Because of this profusion of differing words, both static and dynamic, I have chosen the word 'transition' as a somewhat neutral 'umbrella-word', general enough to contain within itself all these concepts that we are familiar with. I believe that this one word can contain within itself not just the static concepts, but also the dynamic concepts which indicate and even outline the possibility of change in our spiritual lives.

I have presented the common words above in a roughly ascending scale, even if the choice is arbitrary. My choice is not based on a detailed knowledge of the theology of these concepts, but rather on my attempt to organise them even a little. I thereby refer to them quickly and pass on, to concentrate on my main interest which is that of my new-found understanding of the development and growth in the spiritual life of Catholics.

Transition – How

The Catholic Church offers many spiritual exercises, capable of enhancing our transition process. But I sometimes think that specific reference to the details of the improvement of our spiritual lives is an aspect of our religion which is somewhat neglected.

One reason that could explain this neglect is the fact that externally, nothing in our genuine religious practice has to change, in order to make room for transition. This is because our actual transition process takes place precisely through our daily practice of our Catholic faith, with the helps that are available within it.

The source of the fundamental help for the transition process is of course the total spiritual power of Jesus, now delegated to the Catholic Church through the ministry of the Holy Spirit. The Church's sacramental system is the apex and outlet of that power of Jesus now reaching us through the Holy Spirit. It reaches us even when we are born in Original Sin. But by our baptism we are very quickly introduced to our initial reception of the effects of the Good News, and thereby to the possibilities for spiritual development.

The sacramental system is in turn supplemented by all the devotions that are available to us as Catholics. And the different spiritualities of the Church make up the traditional fund of knowledge and guiding wisdom of the Catholic Church by giving us various ways which assist us in our seeking and applying to ourselves these powers of the sacraments and the sacramentals.

All of these are necessary elements in the term 'transition', our 'umbrella-term' for our process of advancing in our spiritual life.

The Sacraments

Part Two of our *'Catechism of the Catholic Faith'* discusses in great detail the backbone of our Catholicism – the Sacraments.

The Sacraments each give me timely and appropriate boosts of God's grace as I wend my way through the demands of my life situation in this episode and interlude of my eternal existence, coming as I did from God, and finding my way back to Him through Jesus.

The Sacramentals

In our Catholic devotions, apart from the actual Sacraments, we have so many practices found mainly and sometimes only in the Roman Catholic faith. We have our special devotion to Mary. We sprinkle blessed water. We accept ashes on our foreheads as a sign of our entry into the penitential season of Lent as preparation for Easter. We wear not just crosses but other medals. As we passed outside a Catholic church, we were accustomed to paying some sign of respect to the Real Presence of Jesus within. We remember our dead and intercede for them. We make no secret of offering up our sufferings to God in the light of and union with the sufferings of Jesus.

There is an almost endless variety of them. And all over the Catholic world there are variations in them. But, as well as being held in high regard, what they have in common is that when we carry them out publicly, we publicly identify ourselves as Catholic.

For me, every one of our various Catholic religious devotions and all of the various kinds of non-sacramental assistance that I can receive from the Catholic Church are in some way the farthest reaches of God's Revelation and God's graces, reaching me via my Catholic faith!

So, as we use each of them appropriately, we are thereby taking one more tiny step in our transition process.

Essentials versus 'Optional Extras'

Those of us who were fortunate enough to be convinced and comfortable in all aspects of our Catholicism always recognise the differing levels of importance between sacraments and sacramentals. We knew what was essential to our Catholic faith. We knew equally well what were 'optional extras'. We took all of them for granted, the devotions we ourselves used and the ones we didn't – and perhaps didn't even like! But even if by habit we were taking them for granted, for convinced Catholics, each devotional practice woven into our daily round was like a tiny wavelet coming all the way from the infinity of our Triune God, through the Church, and culminating in whatever form the devotional behaviour took, as if it was the final rush of God's infinity, available to us at our very feet.

Scripture

The Sacraments are the approved sources or outlets in our faith so that Catholics can have valid and approved access to the power and the effects of the Revelation that has been offered to us. This power was won for us by Jesus and is made available to us through the empowerment by Jesus of the Roman Catholic Church.

Scripture is the selection of writings endorsed by the Church as inspired. And of course, Scripture and the Sacraments and the original power of the Church from which the Sacraments come must all be consistent with one another.

One day may years ago, I went swimming in nearby Lough Swilly, an inlet of the Atlantic Ocean. While musing over the sight of the challenging waves, I thought of them as being analogous to our Catholic Sacraments.

The graces of the Sacraments were available to me in much the same way that the waves of Lough Swilly were available to me. After all, I always had to make the decision to go to get contact with the waves. They did not come to me! Apart from our infant baptism, it is the same with the Sacraments.

Then, when I encountered the waves, I had to conform myself to their power! I must do so too when dealing with our Sacraments. And, no matter how much I enjoyed swimming, and no matter how much I benefited from my encountering the waves, my encounters happened only sometimes, and even

then, only for a short time. After all, while I benefited from the sea and its waves, I did not live my
life in the sea. Indeed, my times on the beaches of
Lough Swilly were most pleasant. But that time was
an interlude in the main business of my developing
existence. This is the perspective I always main-
tained, that my swim was a help to the physical
health I needed and employed in meeting the chal-
lenges of my daily life.

After giving the appropriate importance due to the
main waves, I then also remember the tiny wavelets.
Even on the calmest day, with no great waves possible, they continually rolled onto the beaches and
exhausted themselves at my feet as I stood there.

On reflection, they, too were part of the Atlantic
Ocean, reaching me by their being part of Lough
Swilly. When, in appreciation of the very short
moment of their existence I turned my attention to
them, that part of the Atlantic Ocean thereby became
mine!

By calling up this one memory, I seem to be
momentarily able to combine a number of apparent
contradictories (even though I cannot yet understand
them by having direct and complete experience of
them). But, as a result of being able to refer to this
memory at will, I confirm once again my acceptance
and savour once again my experience that, just by
being the human person I am, I stand at the interface
between the finite and the infinite.

This procedure takes me a little distance along the
road I wish to travel – but not all the way to complete
knowledge. In the absence of my knowing all that I
would like to know, it convinces me that my present
experience and still partial understanding of reality is
consistent with the truth of the Christian Revelation
and my faith in it.

When we become aware not merely that we should make the Good News our own, but also how to do it better than before, our spiritual life becomes active and vibrant. When we know how, and act upon that knowledge, we are deliberately and intelligently engaging in the development of our spiritual dimension by which we are prepared for union with and life in the Trinitarian God, through Jesus, because of Jesus, after Jesus, along with Jesus – and therefore, somewhat like Jesus!

CHAPTER 9

TRANSITION – THE PARABLE OF THE SOWER

While all of Scripture has as its purpose the advancement of our spiritual well-being and development in the various areas of our needs, there is one section of Scripture which strikes me as giving us an over-all picture of what I have called 'the Transition Process'. This is the Parable of the Sower going out to sow seed in the field.

For my purposes, I am using the version in the Gospel of St Mark, chapter four, verses three to nine, because of the logical order of the presentation of the numbers in the second part of the parable.

In the Jerusalem Bible, the parable is presented as follows:

Imagine a sower going out to sow. Now it happened that, as he sowed, some of the seed fell on the edge of the path and the birds came and ate it up. Some seed fell on rocky ground, where it found little soil; and sprang up straightaway, because there was no depth of earth, and when the sun came up, it was scorched, and, not having any roots, it withered away. Some seed fell into thorns and the thorns grew up and choked it, and it produced no crop. And some seeds fell into rich soil and, growing tall and strong, produced crop, and yielded thirty-, sixty-, even a hundred-fold.[1]

The words of Scripture have their own unique spiritual power. But we have to contribute our own little human help in tapping into that power for ourselves. We do so by bringing to bear on the parable whatever added insight and understanding we can gather.

Parable Format

Scripture reaches us through the medium of many formats. We are dealing here with one of these formats, that of a parable. There are parables in all languages, used as a method of teaching. To see how and to what extent we are being taught in this particular parable, it may be worth taking a moment to remind ourselves both of the possibilities and the limitations of the format that a parable is made up of and makes use of.

Straightaway in this parable we can see the lesson that is being taught. The main message is obvious. But while the main message is obvious, different details of the parable can be focused on by different readers or hearers according to differing needs and circumstances. Such flexibility is an added dimension to the usefulness of a parable. Because of its flexibility, there can be differing benefits to different users from the same parable.

[1] Mark 4:3–9.

Jesus explained the parable in its simplest form to the Apostles, in private. We must therefore first note the same timeless lesson given to the Apostles.

But then, in accordance with our own modern-day abilities, with its high standard of education, we can reasonably be expected to go farther than those to whom Jesus preached directly in His Semitic fashion. We can do so by using our Greek way of thinking.

Analysis of the Parable

A cursory glance will show that the parable has two sections, with three divisions in each section.

By analysis, we can see that each of the three divisions in the first section represented a fixed attitude or pattern of action of a certain type of person. These are negative, and are non-fruitful in varying degrees. In the last analysis, each is a failure. In the first division, we start with total hopeless failure. In the second, failure could possibly be avoided, but is not. In the third, there seems to be success, but the failure lies in the fact that the preliminary success is lost.

Then in the second section, there is a change of tone in the parable. Jesus now gives an outline of what is possible, namely that there can be varying degrees of success. Implied in the given figures are the labels of the 'thirty-fold' being 'notable', the 'sixty-fold' being 'wonderful', and the 'hundred-fold' being 'total success'.

Yet, when we think about it, only the possibility of different degrees of success is indicated. There is really nothing in the parable about the nature of this success. We only know that this success (or the lack of it in the first section) applies to our religion, our response to the Good News of Jesus.

So in the first section, we have three negative or unsuccessful outcomes. Each of these is a concrete example, well within our capacity to comprehend from our experience.

In the second section, we also have three outcomes, but this time successful. And we get the concrete example of fruitfulness, namely the possibility of different degrees of spiritual development of the Good News in all its magnitude, indicated by the symbolism of the different numbers.

Appication to Spiritual Transition

After highlighting the very obvious features of the parable, I sum them up as follows.

Coming under an 'umbrella' description of spirituality, we have six levels concerning success or the lack of it – three negative and three positive.

We must of course remember that in the parable, each is initially seen solely as a presentation of the considered and chosen spirituality of a total person. Yet the dynamism of change by conversion and improvement and development is not thereby ruled out. Even in the three divisions of the failures of the first section, actual change and improvement, while not clearly stated, are at least implied by the very existence of something different and better.

But in the second section, change and improvement and development are quite specifically referred to, by the numerical description of improved levels of productivity in the ears of corn. So the parable is showing that there are different levels of spirituality. The parable teaches us to us to draw the conclusion that we should avoid the mistakes illustrated in each section of the first division and aim for the very best of the second section.

Limitations of the Parable

The parable does not give specific details about whether it is possible to pass from one division to the next. Yet such a passage is still implied in the setting of the parable in the context of the natural growth that takes place when seed is planted.

And more importantly, the parable as presented therefore really tells us nothing about how this passing from one state to another might be done in our spiritual lives.

The information that we would be looking for in this regard is of course contained in the informational contents of other parts of the Good News. But in this age of instant satisfactions, of processed foods and TV dinners, we like to have the contents of Scripture presented to us in ways which quickly and conveniently sum up those same contents of the other parts of the Good News.

When I first came across the teachings of St Teresa of Avila, I thought of them as having all the advantages for my spiritual life that convenience foods offer me in my physical life. Here in her teaching was a relatively simple presentation from someone who had been extremely successful in her spiritual life – successful enough to have been created a Doctor of the Universal Church. Her teaching was what we would describe nowadays as a 'case-study' of the success implied as possible in the Parable of the Sower.

The spiritual benefits and effects of the Parable of the Sower and of our Catholic sacramental system do not depend on our having the specific knowledge embodied in the teaching of St Teresa. But such knowledge, even of the possibilities for our spiritual lives too can be an encouragement and help in the ordinary routine and methodology of our present on-going spiritual lives and spirituality.

CHAPTER 10

TRANSITION – ST TERESA OF AVILA

That different levels of spiritual growth are available to us, as in the Parable of the Sower, is in itself good news. But having received this good news, being the kind of people that we are, it is only to be expected that we would like to know more.

Can we go further than the points we have reached as designated in the Parable of the Sower which best show where we have reached in our spiritual lives? Can we do so by getting other, more detailed outlines, not merely of the possibility that there could be different levels of spirituality for me, but of the possibility of growing from the lower to the higher?

I found that we could! I found this because it happened in my case.

And if it happened in my case, it may very well have already happened in your case, too. Or if not, it still could happen!

Spiritual Development

My spiritual development in this particular manner happened this way. In 1983, when I had some time on my hands during home leave, almost as an after-thought a friend casually offered me the loan of a book, giving it no greater endorsement than his comment that I might like to look through it. The book was *The Interior Castle Explored*,[1] by Sister Ruth Burrows, a Carmelite nun. This, the first of her several books, is an introduction to, a presentation and a critique of, the teachings of St Teresa of Avila[2] as contained in St Teresa's final book, *The Interior Castle*.

My little bit of dipping previously into the original works of St Teresa – written for her nuns – I had found rather daunting. The reports and descriptions of raptures and levitations and other spiritual phenomena were away beyond not merely my experience but the experience of anyone I knew. Yet Ruth Burrows' presentation and explanations had of course to refer to and take her readers through the same descriptions by St Teresa of the special graces granted to her in the sixteenth century. So, not having heard much about her that I could remember from the seminary apart from her name and her dates, I was most pleasantly surprised when Ruth Burrows presented all of this to me, one of her readers, in forms and descriptions which are in fact applicable to all of us.

This book by Ruth Burrows opened my eyes to the possibility of seeing more clearly what levels of spiri-tuality there could be. And indeed, thereby seeing what Christianity itself can and should be!

---

[1] Ruth Burrows, *Iterior Castle Explored*, Sheed & Ward/Veritas Publications, 1981.

[2] St Teresa was a Spanish Carmelite nun, born in 1515 and died in 1582. She was declared a Doctor of the Church on 27 September, 1970.

For me, by my reading of this book, Christianity was no longer something static but had become actually and verifiably dynamic! This impression was confirmed for me when I later saw some parallel between the teaching of St Teresa and the teaching of the Parable of the Sower (which is why I have reviewed this parable in such detail).

Different Approaches and Presentations

There is of course quite a noticeable difference in approach between the parable and the ideas of St Teresa, presented as what we would now call 'a case study'. Yet these two approaches in fact complement each other by each illuminating in different ways what are different possibilities for our spiritual lives.

In the parable, there is an unmistakably stark challenge, coming from its Semitic way of thinking with its 'Either-Or' pattern. This obvious 'Either-Or' presentation of the possibilities for spiritual development are highlighted in the tension between the lack of success in the first section and the possibility of success in the second.

Such a stark challenge is perhaps the most basic and most simple model of spirituality that we have. But this very Semitic-style starkness serves the purpose very well of reminding us of the urgency and the imperative need first of all to avoid obvious obstacles, delays and mistakes in our spiritual lives and, more than that, to teach us in the second part to seek for ourselves what is available in the way of spiritual development.

Traditional Three Stages Model

For many years in the Catholic Church there had been a very traditional model for spirituality. Spirituality had been seen as having three stages: the 'Purgative Way' (or stage), the ' Illuminative Way' and the 'Unitive Way'. These three stages make up a simple and effective theory of spirituality. These markers were always seen as a guide to the application and development of Scripture. Traditional as they are, this classification of stages in the spiritual life is still basic and true and useful.

St Teresa's teaching has advantages which include and then go beyond the advantages of this traditional three-stage system. The advantage lies in her presentations being in fact a case-study of herself as she reached the Unitive Way. St Teresa's approach is more 'Both-And' than the 'Either-Or' of the parable. Because she does refer to the bottom of the ladder (the Purgative Way), with her presentation, she takes us through the three traditional stages of Purgative, Illuminative, and Unitive Way in much greater detail than had been available heretofore.

From the very beginning, St Teresa takes for granted and emphasises the possibilities that, no matter where we are starting from, there can and should be improvement, development, and growth in our relationship with God as the paramount purpose of our living in this world. So while still presenting the same basics of Christianity, this kind of presentation should thereby prove much more acceptable to the modern-day reader than the starker, simpler three-stage model, presented in theory and not as an actual case-study.

Starting

The only reason for writing that St Teresa had was her intention to describe by teaching (under obedience) from her own experience what can be possible in the matter of our union with God 'even in this world'.[3] Some aspects of the individual starting points of all of us are described by the parable terminology of 'stony ground'. Yet from that starting-point, no matter what, the Christian message of the Good News is that we can be willing to work up systematically (by the grace of God) to all that St Teresa had to say about union with God, even in this present phase of our existence.

St Teresa was writing for Carmelite nuns – still human beings like ourselves, each with their personal 'stony ground'. Since she was writing for Carmelite nuns, she did not start with the kind of 'stony ground' that we know. The standard of the 'stony ground' she put forward was at a level appropriate for Spanish nuns of her time. And since she was inspired to see the need for some reform among those nuns, her life's work was to carry out this reform for the nuns who wished to join her in it.

St Teresa was very much aware of the kind of 'stony ground' that called for reform in the structuring of the Carmelite way of life that she and her sisters were following. But I believe that when her understanding and experience about the farthest reaches of Christianity is applied to others, and not just to nuns, we can adapt her teaching in these matters so as to apply it appropriately to ourselves.

---

[3] 1 John 4:17.

Union with God

Catholicism holds out for us the hope and expectation that union with God after this life is possible. But union with God as far as possible, 'even in this world' is what is described here in this particular work. And that is the purpose endorsed by the Catholic Church in its approval of the Teachings of St Teresa by declaring her a 'Doctor (or Teacher) of the Universal Church'. So it is also basic Christianity that not just union with God *after* this life, but even union with God *in* this life as far as possible, should be our Christian purpose, as well as expectation of union with Him in the next life. Therefore, in genuine Catholicism we should not just take for granted this opportunity as if it were merely an 'optional extra', and by doing so, thereby overlook and neglect it.

We still of course need to make use of all the assistance given to us by the Catholic Church. Many of these are particularly useful and helpful at our starting points. But if we are to go farther, we need to take an intelligent and informed interest in our spiritual lives, with their different starting points. For that, we need to know that such theory exists and then absorb as much theory as we can, to motivate and guide us in the process of developing spiritually.

Even a static understanding of the teaching of St Teresa fills that need.

A dynamic application to ourselves of this teaching is our actual entering consciously and responsibly into the Transition Process!

St Teresa's *Interior Castle*

The special ability that St Teresa was privileged to have was that first of all she experienced a very special spiritual life. Like so many others, this was accompanied by much suffering. But added to that, St Teresa was specially gifted in her ability to put her spiritual experiences into words, for the guidance and benefit of others. By being so, her descriptions are a 'case study' of the spiritual experiences she had been graced with.

It seemed to her that her soul (and ours) was like a king's castle but it was as if the castle was so precious that it was in fact a precious diamond. Being a great castle, it had many rooms. And the benefit to us of such a castle is that it would be possible to progress through these rooms until we could reach the throne-room, where the King dwells. The throne room of the castle is the inner recesses of our souls. And in that throne-room of our souls, there already resides the King – God Almighty.

But our entering into this 'interior castle' is considered to be our starting this journey as if we were only in the courtyard – or even outside! Neither is a very attractive place to be. Her similes for such a situation describe the state and condition of the soul of a person who is careless about, or actually guilty of, sinning. This is the 'stony ground' of the parable and the Purgative Way of the traditional theory.

Most of us do not have the impression that we have reached the Throne Room of the King. We can even have the impression of still being 'in the court-yard'. Yet the message for us is that, even if we are only starting here 'in the courtyard', it is possible that we too can reach that Throne Room and be welcomed by the King. From that time on, we would thereafter dwell in His presence – 'even in this world'

But start we must! And that, in another word, is Transition!

CHAPTER 11

ST TERESA OF AVILA –
THE MANSIONS

As we journey towards the centre that St Teresa described as 'The Throne Room of His Majesty', there are various stages.

St Teresa uses the simile 'mansions' to indicate and classify and then describe these stages. Passing through them one after another in her simile is the Illuminative Way of traditional theory.

Our business is to have the intention to keep going in our co-operation with God's special graces until we too would reach our 'throne room', which would be the constant awareness of the presence of God. And this constant and direct awareness of the presence of God within us is of course the Unitive Way of traditional theory.

'Morados', Mansions, Stages

Before we look more closely at the essence of the actual teaching of St Teresa, I wish to highlight one of the earliest and most important points that Ruth Burrows has emphasised.

Ruth Burrows pointed out that we should under-

stand the word 'mansion' (the usual translation
from the Spanish word *'morados')* as applying not
just to the heavenly mansion promised to us by
Jesus[1] or to the 'rooms' in this 'castle', but even to
the travellers' shelters that were commonplace in
medieval Spain. This is important because St Teresa
divided her descriptions of the progress of the
spiritual life into seven of these 'mansions' or
'morados'.

By doing so, St Teresa wished to emphasise the
dynamic nature of the possible developments in our
spiritual life by emphasising that it is our business to
move from one mansion or room to another, by spiritual development, on our inward journey towards
union with our King.

Youth Hostels

As I wondered how I too could emphasise this
point, I remembered hearing a description of his
holiday in Australia by a student who had spent his
vacation travelling there. He told me that the
Australian tourist industry had made special, very
attractive arrangements for people like himself. In
Queensland he was able to buy a ticket for a bus
route which went south from there to Melbourne.
He could get off the bus on this route at any of the
stops where there were youth hostels. He could
stay in the area for whatever time he wished,
and then board the next bus and continue his
journey.

It struck me that such an arrangement of convenient youth hostels would be a modern-day version

[1] John 14:2.

of the *'morados'* of medieval Spain that St Teresa referred to and that Ruth Burrows had highlighted for her readers.

By this distinction St Teresa was emphasising the point that our stay in any of the mansions less than the seventh should only be temporary. It should therefore be the attitude and mind-set of genuine and committed Christians that our stay in any of the preliminary spiritual states that she described should be temporary.

In other words, we should be open to change and development and advancement in our spiritual lives. For that, we should seek and welcome any basic knowledge that would help us as we seek and welcome such spiritual growth.

Application

All that might be all very fine for theory about the spirituality of others and for guidance in pastoral work, but 'first things first'. As I read and re-read Ruth Burrows, I asked myself how these teachings could apply to me. To my amazement and delight, I found that I could remember an experience in my life when I was already thirty years ordained, which seemed to match her description of the Fourth Mansion.

If that were true, could something at that level of spirituality be true of me?

Well, after thirty years as a missionary priest, why not!

Application to us

We hear of and believe in such wonders as happened to saints like St Teresa, and we can understand that the achievement of this transforming union is the whole aim and purpose of the Rule that guides the lives of Carmelite Sisters. This Rule, and others like it, are intended to have as their only aim that people will be brought into this kind of union with God in as far as is possible for human beings in this life.

Hopefully, we dutifully applaud.

Regretfully, we may at the same time be saying to ourselves: 'This is not for me!'

But we are told by the wisdom of the Church that transforming union is what is needed so as to be worthy of Heaven! And by canonising lay people, the Church has highlighted the example of people who are not formally in religious life yet people who have achieved this end. And the example is for this purpose, namely that we recognise that implicit in our desire to get to Heaven is our task of reaching some form of transforming union.

Later? or Now?

If we take time to think of what Heaven is going to be, we will probably come to the conclusion that it is our task to achieve transforming union either in this life or in the next.

And better – much, much better – in this life!

Some aspects of the starting points of all of us may be described by the parable terminology of 'stony ground'. Yet from that starting point, the Christian message is that we are brought up systematically towards all that St Teresa has to say about union with

God. The only reason for writing that St Teresa had was her intention to describe, and thereby to teach from her own experience, what can be possible in the matter of our union with God 'even in this world'.[2]

Of Applcation to all?

Primarily, what St Teresa wrote seemed only for enclosed Carmelite nuns. In this regard, Ruth Burrow states that it was 'a disputed question as to whether the call to the mystical life is for all'.[3]

Ruth Burrows settled that question definitively when she went on to write:

> Surely the message of the New Testament is that union with God, divine intimacy, familiarity, unheard of privilege, is what man is for; it is the promise of the Father offered in Jesus and for which He died. We are called to be sons in the Son, heirs of God, because [we are] co-heirs with Christ, sharing in the divine nature, filled with the fullness of God.[4]

Ruth Burrows was in practice stating that what was available to Carmelite Sisters is available to all. I believe that statement to be true in my own case, because, once I adverted to my own experience, I found that it was in the process of becoming true.

That such material came my way I consider to be the second of the two major insights I referred to in my introduction because I benefited so much from

[2] 1 John 4:17.
[3] Ruth Burrows, *Interior Castle Explored*, p. 40.
[4] Ibid. p. 41.

them. But as well as coming to an appreciation of how I too had benefited along these lines, my digging into this matter showed me that the circumstance that I happened to be a missionary priest was irrelevant.

CHAPTER 12

MANSIONS ONE TO THREE

After my introduction to the teaching of St Teresa of Avila and applying that teaching to myself, it was natural that I wanted to convey to others the spiritual riches I had found there.

It is of course true that all that I had learned would be equally available to anyone who read the same books that I had read. But in the time immediately after I had had my chance to read, the 'others' of my concern were first of all the university-level students in the school complex to which I had at that time been assigned for campus ministry. Later, they were my parishioners, mostly in rural settings. Neither of these groups had access to the books that I had access to, and even if they had, those books would not have been suitable.

In the absence of books, the first thing I had to do was to prepare a summary and simplification of what I had learned, and prepare mimeographed hand-outs for seminars and other talks.

Simplification

I always started my presentations by first introducing the Parable of the Sower. I then went on to point out the two main divisions in the parable. The first division referred first to the stony ground, then the shallow soil, and then the weed-infested soil. The second division consisted of the numerical descriptions 'thirtyfold', 'sixtyfold', and 'one hundredfold'. I then introduced St Teresa and her teaching.

To begin my actual simplification, I pointed out the two major divisions in both the parable and in her group of seven mansions. The three mansions in the first division all come under the general heading:

'I Let God be God in Me'

Now. this is not just something which is good in itself, but something that is necessary. But as yet, it is of no great degree of goodness or sanctity ... After all, I cannot stop God being God. Neither can I stop Him from being God in me!

Mansion One

However, the whole point of St Teresa's teaching is that we can carry out this good and necessary duty at three levels of intensity. And the first level is the first mansion. I can permit God to be 'God in me' to happen only at the very lowest level.

The first level or mansion is distinguished from the other two in the same division by having a qualifying statement added to it, namely:

'I let God be God in me as Little as Possible'

We could recall for a moment the description of this lowest level as given in the Parable of the Sower. If and when I find that the description of the First Mansion applies to me (or, better, applies to certain aspects of my response to God), I can describe myself and my minimal spirituality and the reaction of my soul in that matter as 'stony ground'.

Or I could use a modern-day simile and say that I am willing merely to 'pay the fire insurance' against the pains of Hell. It is usual with the matter of paying fire insurance, that I do so only with the greatest reluctance, and simply because it is unavoidable. This is precisely the spirit in which even the minimum service is rendered to God.

Zero

But, having said that, another modern-day division has to be given consideration.

In the faith-filled times and surroundings of St Teresa, this statement 'I let God be God in me' was, by-and-large, applicable to all Catholics. But in our present day and present religious climate, can we say this with confidence about all the people around us? When we look around us and hear what many people are openly saying, we cannot make this statement.

If we say that we cannot, then, sadly, we really have to add another division, lower than the first mansion, that of zero.

For those of us who believe, the main purpose of underlining the possibility described by the symbol zero is to give us an added urgency to our consideration of these matters. We too could be in danger of being sucked insidiously into such a stance. And because we are not, we can consequently see that it is a tragedy that from the pinnacle of His material creation, us human beings, God is not getting the response He deserves. And God, even when He became Man, did not get the response He deserved.[1]

Mansion One – Philippine Setting

In the Philippine setting of my ministry, paying insurance was not as common as it is in Europe. In view of that, I used to give another example, more appropriate to my situation and much more easily understood, namely the example of the *'puro Katolikong olitawo'*.

'Olitawo' is the designation in the Cebuano Visayan dialect given to young men who are not yet married. While not entirely implying that they are irresponsible, in Philippine culture there is a great tolerance of this trait in these young men.

The designation *'puro Katoliko'* means 'pure Catholic'. It is of application to others as well as to the young unmarried men.

I was very familiar with this type of Filipino Catholic. When I asked them about their religion, they would invariably describe themselves as 'pure Catholic'. It took me a while to grasp the nuance of such a designation.

---

[1] Remembrancec of our capacity to have compassion for Jesus who suffered so much and so openly for us, and even compassion for the Trinty of God, because of the hardness of people's hearts in refusing to respond to the goodness of the Trinity, is the basis for the on-going Catholic devotion to the Sacred Heart of Jesus.

'Catholic' yes! But what was their actual practice of our Catholic religion?

On examination of their 'practice' of the faith, I discovered what it usually meant.

Their 'practice of their Catholic faith' could consist of as little as two activities. The first would be their attending the Good Friday procession. Most of their time as spectators of the procession was spent in looking out for the very devout, very demure, but very pretty unmarried girls in the procession. This would be true until the *'Santa Entierro'* (the statue of the Body of the Dead Christ in a glass coffin which was the reason for and heart of the procession) almost reached them. They would then hurriedly make an attempt at blessing themselves, drop their eyes, and wait until the carriage carrying the coffin and statue had passed. Then they would resume their look-out for the best-looking girls in the procession.

As a second 'practice' of their Catholic faith, these young men also had their special brand of devotion to the Holy Souls.

Devotion to the souls of the departed is universal all over the Philippines. There was the peculiarity that in the northern regions of the Philippines, the special day for Mass attendance and visiting the cemeteries to attend individual blessings of the graves was 1 November, whereas in our area in the south, it was 2 November. But in each place, and on the appropriate night, groups of these *'olitawo'* would arrange to spend the night before 1 or 2 November in the cemetery – with bottles of rum to keep them fortified!

For the *'puro Katoliko'* young men, anything like Mass attendance or confession was out of the question. But equally, there was never any possibility of their joining any other religion. After all, they were '*puro Katoliko!*' This was their unashamed label for themselves – and indeed, their boast!

My listeners were aware that such 'practice of the Catholic faith' was typical for so many of these young men. So my reference to this as an example of first mansion spirituality was usually greeted with a tolerant smile, and never challenged as an example of the first mansion of St Teresa which could make an inpact.

Stony Ground

'Stony ground?' 'Yes' – and 'No!'

'Yes!' When judged by what is accepted as the minimum of religious practice for Catholics, even in the Philippines (with disproportionately large numbers of people for the very few priests available), what these young men were doing was undeniably 'stony ground'.

But at the same time 'No!' They would never cease to call themselves Catholic. They would never join any other religion. This trait at least was positive, even if only by being an absence of what could have been worse!

Transition

Could any transition from Original Sin to Union with God be detected?

'No' – and 'Yes!'

They may not have seriously started or gone far on their spiritual journey after their baptism. But they had not abandoned the journey. They had not denied that there is such a journey which should be made –

even though they themselves at that stage of their lives had not seriously started on it. In view of these considerations, they had not abandoned the possibility at least of transition. And in the older people, they had examples of such transition. Regretfully, we are not able to say the same about many in modern Europe!

Comparison

Only when I have encountered so many reports here in Europe and in the world of the West of people who vociferously deny that there is such a journey and act accordingly, have I come to see the value of what so many Filipinos have held on to, no matter how small. I am very confident that God, before giving His final judgement, will take into consideration the lack of advantages and the multitude of disadvantages that these young Filipino men had to grow up under and live with.

We must also remember that this 'stony ground' of the still irresponsible young unmarried men of the Philippines is a far cry from the 'stony ground' of religious novices in a medieval Spanish convent. St Teresa was writing for the latter. As a result, in reading her original teachings, we might be tempted to think that even her starting point is beyond our spiritual capacities. So I have deliberately included this description of how far I believe this concept of 'stony ground' could be stretched.

I do so to spark off in my readers some sense of urgency for seeking in themselves what is the 'stony ground' in their particular lives. And a sense of hope, no matter how far down the scale of religious belief and practices they may have to go!

Mansion Two

When using this example of the young unmarried men attending the Good Friday procession, I always stated the obvious. Girl-watching is hazardous to bachelorhood! I continue my example to the point where the typical young man does get married. Because of his new responsibilities and force of circumstances, I always asked my listeners to imagine a very typical scenario.

Because of his getting married and now having to support a family, it would not be unusual for such a young man to become a tenant of a small area of coconut land, usually belonging to a relation of his or of his wife. This would mean leaving the town and living in a *barrio*.

In many *barrios*, there is a regular schedule for monthly Mass taking place, on a weekday. In due course, the first child of this couple arrives and can be baptised at the monthly Mass. But the young father does not attend. Nor for his second child.

But when the third child has been born, I suggest a change. The young man has become more responsible. He is now attending the monthly Mass perhaps a total of three times in a year. And he does attend the baptism of his third child. When he is now prepared to do these things, his religious state could now be described as:

'I let God be God in me more than before'

In the Parable of the Sower, this is described by the example of 'little soil'.

Mansion Three

After more time has passed, another level of spirituality is reached. The once-young man has now become very responsible. Over the years, he has in fact become the leader for the affairs of the *'capilla'* or chapel of the *barrio*. And as one priest is replaced by another, the name of this particular leader is passed on as being 'a pillar of the Church' in that barrio.

In this way, the man of my example has reached the third level, namely that:

'I let God be God in me as much as I possibly can'

Now this seems high praise for anyone, anywhere. And in every parish I ever served in, I have found such good, loyal, dependable people, sometimes leaders in the religious affairs of the *barrio* and always supporters of the Catholic priest whoever he may be.

'Good – but not Sufficient'

It is only when we get to this point that the uniqueness of Christian spirituality is highlighted for us by St Teresa. AND by the Parable of the Sower! It is in accordance with each of these sources that we can, surprisingly, evaluate this Third Mansion as being 'Good – but not sufficient!'

This is so only because the potential fruitfulness of the rest of the Parable of the Sower and the potential success of reaching the Throne Room of the King have not yet taken place.

It is in accordance with the pastoral care of the Church that credit must always be given for progress that has taken place. But without denying that, the

Semitic pattern of thinking in the Parable of the Sower points out that while the seed of the sower has indeed fallen on fertile soil, weeds can still grow up and choke off the product of the seed. The leaving behind of the example of natural growth and the substitution of the uncharacteristic description by mathematical means implies that for further development, new thinking and imagining serves us best.

St Teresa sees this to be true. She sees that there is a potential for spiritual development available to us even beyond the good habits built up and practised so as to qualify people to be in the Third Mansion. St Teresa emphasises that these same good habits could actually mask the unrealised potential. In fact, in the scriptural terms of the Parable of the Sower, improperly used, they could even be the weeds!

CHAPTER 13

MANSION FOUR PART I

I have just re-read the chapter on the 'Fourth Mansion: Part I' by Ruth Burrows in her book 'The Interior Castle Explored'. Whatever the difficulties in reading it for the first time, my re-reading confirms for me that this particular chapter of the book effected a change for me for ever – and for the better – of my picture and understanding of Christianity. This change came about for me by my becoming aware of having entered and thereby received the graces of the Fourth Mansion. That is why I still find it worthwhile to re-read what St Teresa had to say, as interpreted for me by Ruth Burrows. Each re-reading confirms my conviction of having received this grace.

Supernatural Prayer

At the beginning of her first chapter of two on the Fourth Mansion, Ruth Borrows brings us immediately to the essence of the change that happens in the Fourth Mansion when she quotes directly

from St Teresa, that we 'begin to touch the supernatural'.[1]

When first reading this, my reaction to that statement was mild surprise. Isn't all prayer said to be
'supernatural'? Especially when we are told specifically by St Paul that 'we do not even know how to
pray but ... the Spirit Himself is pleading for us'.[2]

The same traditional Catholic teaching is presented
to us when we are taught the technical term of 'actual
grace', the grace which is needed for us to respond in
any way to God. Response to God very obviously
includes our consenting and deciding to pray, so
when we pray, we have been touched by supernatural, actual grace and have responded to it. And our
Sacraments, including our baptism while still infants,
are channels of the supernatural. St Teresa and the
people she was writing for knew all that. But she
wanted to teach what she knew of the higher reaches
of contemplative prayer.

She herself seemed to have a very special and
unique kind of self-knowledge and awareness about
the way of praying which she had experienced. This
was knowledge and awareness which her nuns did
not have. And neither do we. But since she told them
– and now us – about it, we too can benefit from that
special knowledge of hers.

The technical name for this kind of prayer is
'infused prayer' and the name 'infused contemplation' is given to the special grace that is needed for
this advanced prayer.

St Teresa herself acknowledged that there were
already many excellent books available on prayer for

[1] Ruth Burrows, *The Interior Castle Explored*, p. 36.
[2] Rom. 8:26–7.

her nuns. But she herself had been given knowledge through direct experience of the advanced stages of prayer that she did not find in those books. Hence, in obedience to her spiritual director, she undertook to convey to her nuns – and also to us – the possibilities available to those of us who are serious about praying and thereby developing our personal relationship with God through Jesus.

Infused Prayer

This development of our personal relationship with Jesus as a result of our receiving the grace of contemplation shows itself in our infused prayer – an added area of direct influence of God within us individually and personally. This results in an added capacity for our contact with God. This capacity is something new, something that is brought into being directly by God Himself. (Ruth Burrows has emphasised this point repeatedly throughout her book.[3])

Clarifications

This 'fourth mansion' experience is our genuine development in prayer. It is this which is 'the crop', indicated in the simplicity of the Parable of the Sower. The Parable of the Sower may be seen as applying to the state of the whole spiritual life in

---

[3] As well as emphasising this point in this chapter on the Fourth Mansion, in the very first chapter of her commentary, Ruth Burrows has devoted time and space to emphasise this idea of spiritual growth by stressing that in spiritual growth 'something new comes into being'.

general of the person. St Teresa's mansions apply more specifically to prayer experience. Just like the successful crop, development in prayer comes into being in its own appropriate time, as a result of perseverance in and faithfulness to prayer on our side, but as a result of God's plan for us and its timing on His side.

Our ordinary, routine, day-to-day life goes on. In it, all Catholics have the standard and essential and basic help of the Catholic Church sacramental system, and many other devotions offered by the Catholic Church. It is a matter of faith that we have a right to expect spiritual results from these apparently ordinary devotions.

But at this stage of our spiritual development, the praying we do as an integral part of our on-going spiritual life changes. The indicators or symptoms of change and development are still only transient. They are not yet the total change. While they may take place without our knowing of them, it is a pity to miss them and to miss the encouragement they can bring, simply because we do not know about them.

The Parable and the Mansion

In the Parable of the Sower, we have the major change from negative to positive when we are presented with the idea of the seed eventually being able to produce its crop. But this does not happen in nature until obstacles are overcome. It is only then that growth will start. We must therefore first of all be prepared to wait. But equally, I believe that we must be prepared to move, by accepting that what was possible for St Teresa and her nuns – (and, apparently for the author of this book)

– is equally possible for the reader.

In the second section of the parable, we are given actual figures indicating the possibility or potential for added growth. We will therefore limit our understanding of the parable and frustrate its application to ourselves if we do not open ourselves to the possibility of being recipients of the added spiritual growth indicated by the progression of these numbers.

In our prayer lives we are not limited to being exactly the same as we always were. When we hear or read about them, or are in any way told about them, there is no reason why we should not look out for the 'symptoms' within ourselves. In itself, this can be potentially dangerous. But the danger is very adequately counteracted if we are always willing to check the validity of our experience by our self-report to a competent spiritual director.

But, sadly, competent and informed spiritual directors are not so easily available to as many Catholics as to us priests. In fact, even for us such spiritual directors are hard to have access to. Hence the need to know even a little, because even the little we can know can be for our own encouragement.

Distinction

Ruth Burrows suggests a 'distinction between what is the mystical encounter itself (which is the essence of the Fourth Mansion graces) and the possible effects of this in the psychic powers ... questions which have absorbed the attention of grave men over the centuries'.[4] Her distinction has succeeded in showing

[4] Ibid. pp. 40–2.

how the graces which came to St Teresa with their many flamboyant effects in her psychic powers can equally be available to us. This is a most important idea because these graces are usually given to us without our being specially gifted with such special psychic powers.

We have always been told by the Church that even what we consider ordinary, mundane, routine, can be given a supernatural value by us through our intentions and by using the various means given to us by the Church. I found that the discussions and explanations of Ruth Burrows all helped to illuminate further this truth already taught by the Church.

For us, therefore, these explanations can thereby more firmly bridge the gap between the wonders of the 'supernatural' that we read about in the lives of the saints and the very ordinary, mundane experiences which are all that we are capable of. So, without a doubt, the apparent limitations in our psychic abilities are no obstacle to the supernatural graces that can still come to us without any wonderful manifestations.

Perspective

What then of the first three mansions?

The standard reached in the Third Mansion seems so high and therefore so satisfying and actually satisfactory. Yet Ruth Burrows has this to say about the Second and Third Mansions:

The second mansion is more like a railway station than a chamber of a castle made for living in. A railway station is for arrivals and departures.[5]
There was a time when I took it for granted that the third mansion represented a first goal, a modest one indeed, but a goal none the less. Now I see it as a stopping-place, somewhere that should not be; we have settled down and made our home in the railway station![6]

To digest this extraordinary statement about the Third Mansion, we should stand back for a moment and ask ourselves what Christianity really wants from us for our eternal benefit. In the New Testament we have a statement of this ultimate aim and final criterion of the development that is possible for us. It is in a statement coming from Jesus Himself: The statement is '... loving as I have loved you.'[7]

So, reaching the Third Mansion is movement and development towards that goal. But it is by no means the goal itself. Undoubtedly, something has been achieved.

We can see what our entry into this mansion has achieved for us in terms of our increased closeness to God when we learn that that our individual and personal efforts involved in these first three mansions can all be described as 'generous preparation'.[8] In the Parable of the Sower we were told that 'some seed fell into thorns and the thorns grew up and choked it'. The thorns would have grown on rich, fertile soil.

[5] Ibid. p. 26.
[6] Ibid. p. 27.
[7] Ibid. p. 42; John 13:34.
[8] Ruth Burrows, *The Interior Castle Explored*, p. 43.

Our 'generous preparation' is that rich, fertile soil, cleared of thorns. But no more than that!

'Generous preparation' is still not yet the crop of our spiritual development. That is why that putting these three mansions into their proper perspective gives us an evaluation as follows: 'Good – but not sufficient.'[9]

[9] Ibid. p. 55.

CHAPTER 14

MANSON FOUR PART II

In simplifying my summary of the remaining mansions, I am showing the same kind of progression that we saw in the Parable of the Sower and then in the first three mansions. To do so for the first three mansions, I gave a general statement applicable to each of the three. I now do the same for the other four mansions.

The general statement applicable to mansions four to seven is:

God makes his presence (not felt but) known in me

There is a major change in these last four mansions similar to the major change in the Parable of the Sower, when the parable referred to results and did so by giving actual numbers instead of details and circumstances about the preparation for these numbers to be realised.

This major change is indicated in the very first word of my summary phrase.

Instead of starting with 'I' as in the first three, the first word here is 'God'.

Because in the Fourth Mansion, there is a new and special emphasis on God.

Ruth Burrows writes:

'Because the mystical encounter is precisely a direct encounter with God Himself.[1]

And:

Infused or mystical contemplation is God in direct contact. God Himself and not a created image of Him, and therefore 'supernatural' in regard to the subject; contacting in a way beyond the ordinary faculties, therefore, supernatural in its mode also ... When we insist that this encounter with God Himself must, of its nature, bypass or transcend our material faculties, we are saying that it must be 'secret' – John of the Cross insists on this – from the intellect that receives it.[2]

All that Ruth Burrows has said in these words is what I have tried to summarise in the phrase 'God makes His Presence ... known'. In parenthesis I have included the phrase '(not felt but)' to make it very clear that this 'knowing' is not the 'knowing' so often claimed by the Charismatics.

Two questions

Ruth Burrows has addressed these 'two burning questions':[3] 'How could this apply to me? If it did, how would I know?'

---

[1] *Interior Castle Explored*, pp. 37–8. Italics are those of Ruth Burrows.
[2] Ibid. p. 38.
[3] Ibid. p. 59.

Her answer to the first of these starts by her asking the further question: 'What is the normal experience of the first mystical graces?'

And she answers: '... that experience will be precisely non-experience in the popular sense of the term ... An encounter has taken place in the depth of being, in the growing point of spirit, and human consciousness, essentially material, can know nothing of it directly'.

The second question is: 'Do those advanced in the spiritual way not know it at all?'

'The answer is that they do know it, but do not know how they know or what they know ... they do not know it at the time it happens but only, looking back, they know it has happened. Sometime in their life they are going to know.'

And:

'Whatever we may feel and think, there is ultimately only one way of knowing that the will has known this union with God, and that is the effects of this prayer and the actions which follow.'[4]

So these effects and these actions are an added dimension to the ordinary service of God that we continue to offer to Him, but now, because of this extra grace from God, somehow better and deeper and more convinced and more intense. This new development, this new action of God, is given the name 'The Grace of Contemplation'.[5]

[4] Ibid. p. 57.
[5] Ibid. p. 38. Ruth Burrows points out that there was a traditinal meaning and application of the word 'contemplaation', which St Teresa of Avila follows. But there can be confusion because in a spiritual direction course, we were told that St Ignatius used the same word 'contemplation' to designate a procedure which differed in some ways from basic meditation.

Possibility of Success

St Teresa believes that 'the greatest number of souls enter these beginnings of infused prayer'.[6] If this be so, then it is important that pertinent information on all this be easily available to all Catholics who are serious about their praying.

In their chapters on the Fourth Mansion, St Teresa, and following her, Ruth Burrows, give such information in their descriptions of the 'Prayer of Quiet'.

Applicable to me?

All that is very well in the kind of theory we can get in books. After reading about it, I asked myself: 'Is it possible for me?' 'Is it applicable for me?' After asking myself these questions, I remembered an incident from a number of years ago which had happened while I was at prayer.

I was on retreat at the time and had just finished reading a section of my daily Office. After a few minutes, I jerked back into self-awareness which I then realised I had momentarily left. As I did so, I was immediately conscious of the fact that in those few moments I had still been praying, unawares. I was praying at a higher level than I myself was ever capable of. Was that a grace of the Fourth Mansion that I was now reading about? For me? Could it be as simple (and in some ways as ordinary) as that?

After re-reading Ruth Burrows on this Fourth Mansion, I considered this to be my first conscious

---

[6] Ibid. p. 71. See also Thomas Dubay, SM, *Fire Within*, Ignatius Press, p. 86.

awareness of the grace of the Fourth Mansion in me.

And why not? After being thirty years ordained, I remembered that previous occasion, even though it was only later that I could compare it with what I had been reading. Apparently it had happened!

CHAPTER 15

THE PRAYER OF QUIET

When we see a technical term like this applied to a situation, we can find it esoteric and off-putting. But the technical term is there because it is an indicator of the sense of understanding and the sense of management and success that privileged souls have had concerning the usual difficulty encountered by people who pray.

Information, encouragement, guidance about this from us priests and other spiritual directors is generally requested from people who have not had this sense of success or of adequate management of their prayer-life. They had in the past been fervent in their prayers and thereby had a sense of accomplishment and satisfaction. Now they have come to a time in their spiritual development when this sense of accomplishment and its accompanying satisfaction have gone. They report: 'I don't seem to be able to pray the way I used to!' And this can be most distressing for them.

The Catholic Church has been the possessor of traditional wisdom concerning this matter. The simplest presentation of this wisdom is in the Ignatian and Jesuit spirituality theory. The term 'consolation' is used to describe the feelings of people who are enjoying satisfaction and their sense of accomplishment in praying, and the term 'desolation' is then used when these encouraging feelings are no longer experienced. Other writers use 'aridity' as the synonym of desolation.

Forced Choice

Basic theory of spirituality has always been emphatic in guiding us in this situation. God is now putting before people the choice they must make:

'Do I want the consolations of God or the God of consolations?'

Naturally they want both, and up until this point they have been getting both.

But it is basic Christian spirituality that for our development, we must be prepared to forego the consolations of God in our praying so as to open ourselves to the advances of the God of consolations – even without these same previous consolations.

In fact, the matter is not in our hands. It is imposed on us by God because it is the usual experience of our entering into 'infused contemplation'. And the results of this testing show up in our praying.

The 'Prayer of Quiet' describes the way that we can continue to pray in this new situation. In fact, it is a concomitant of entry into the Fourth Mansion. It is therefore an added difficulty. But the other side of the coin is this. In this actual experiencing and management of this difficulty, we have a verifiable sign – in fact a 'symptom' – of this entry of ours into the more advanced mansions described in Teresian spirituality.

First Condition

The Prayer of Quiet is not going to happen unless we have two complementary conditions in place.

The first condition is that we are willing to receive any grace that God in His goodness is willing to offer, up to and including this first of the graces of contemplation.

This may seem so obvious as to be hardly worth saying. But Ruth Burrows makes it very clear that there is actually a very great hidden spiritual obstacle here. The hidden obstacle is, amazingly, the hazard of our reaching the Third Mansion. This is so because our natural tendency is to wish to remain in control of our spiritual affairs, so that we can continue to give God all He seems to want. But it must be 'I' who gives!

We find both an example of this problem and an example of the solution in the Parable of the Pharisee and the Tax Collector.

The parable is as follows:

Two men went up to the Temple to pray, one a Pharisee, the other a tax collector. The Pharisee stood there and said this prayer to himself: 'I thank You, God, that I am not grasping, unjust, adulterous, like the rest of mankind, and particularly that I am not like this tax collector here. I fast twice a week; I pay tithes on all I get.

The tax collector stood some distance away, not daring even to raise his eyes to Heaven; but he beat his breast and said: 'God, be merciful to me, a sinner!' This man, I tell you, went home at rights again with God; the other did not. For everyone

who exalts himself will be humbled, but the man
who humbles himself will be exalted'.[1]

When it comes to our understanding of the parable
for its application to ourselves, it is well to note that
the parable follows the Semitic pattern of thought by
giving us the example of 'two men'. We might find
the parable more easily comprehensible if we recognise that, using our Greek way of thinking, we see
that each man in the parable represents a tendency
within each one of us.

In the parable, again as common in Semitic thinking, the two tendencies are portrayed as extreme
cases, as happens in so many parables. As a result,
the extremism may obscure for us what the message
of the parable is for us. The extent of the supercil-
iousness of the Pharisee may mask for us the
message that we must be prepared to surrender
control to God. The abjectness of the response of the
publican may mask the message that God requires
us to approach Him not in abjection but in appropriate humility.

In the Pharisee of the parable, we can see a concrete
example of the spiritual hazard of our being very
willing to serve God, but being very unwilling to give
up our control of that service. In the tax collector, we
can see the complete spiritual poverty which is also
ours in these matters of receiving special graces. In
that example, we can see how we too must be willing
to accept this condition if we are to be privileged by
receiving a higher presence of God Himself in our
souls even in this world.

[1] Luke 18:9–14.

The Pharisee Tendency

The Pharisee tendency towards perfection is not necessarily completely bad. In fact, we need it – but in moderation! It is needed to the extent that we must indeed do all that is possible as the 'generous preparation'[2] which is essential if we are to reach even the Third Mansion. We too must be prepared to put all our best efforts into the behaviour and attitudes that are appropriate for the development of our spiritual lives.

But having done so, we need this gigantic spiritual 'change of gear'. Nothing that we can do can earn for ourselves the right to this grace of contemplation. This is a gift from God. And having done all we can, we need this God-given 'change of gear'. We must then be prepared to open ourselves to God's direct intervention in our spiritual lives, and wait for it to happen in His way and in His good time.

But this does not happen unchallenged. The Pharisee tendency in me can be saying most seductively: 'God, I am so glad that I have my life in order! I do this. I do that. I go to Mass faithfully every day. I treat my morning Mass with the same importance (and even more) with which other people treat their Sunday Mass.'

All of which is fine!

But then comes the hazard!

We can find ourselves going on to say in our own minds: 'God, if You really want more, just let me know! If You want me to go to an evening Mass as well as the morning Mass, just let me know and I will grant that extra service to You most willingly!'

---

[2] Ruth Burrows, *Interior Castle Explored*, p. 54.

The error in all this generosity is that God does not want just our service but our total selves. And if we succumb to the seduction, we are willing to give our total service – but not our total selves!

And our total selves is what God really wants!

The Publican/Tax Collector Tendency

The 'Publican' tendency towards humility can become a natural, logical consequence when we are convinced that a grace such as is on offer at this Fourth Mansion level is very much a gift. We cannot earn a gift. While we do have the power to postpone receiving or to refuse it and even to spurn it, nothing that we can do can earn for ourselves the right to this grace of contemplation.

The corollary to this is that this gift of the grace of contemplation of the Fourth Mansion is something that can come to us only in God's time of choosing – not in ours!

This truth is needed to guide us through the difficulties of what traditional spirituality describes as 'the desert experience'. Jesuit spirituality describes this as 'desolation'. St John of the Cross describes it as 'the dark night of the soul'. The tax collector of the parable stands for the necessity in us that we consent to this experience under whatever name comes to us when we accept that we really have no good works to offer to God which are sufficient to merit this grace, but only our repentance to the extent that I have described in chapters five and six.

But again, even in this, there are the hazards I already referred to in chapter three. I can continue to insist that 'I am not worthy'. And even if in my head

I get over that, I can still find in my heart 'I really do not want!'

So for proper understanding and management of our spiritual lives, we must recognise the existence within us of the tendency towards evil even in its most subtle forms, and learn its management, but at the same time recognise the existence and potential for good within us. We usually have only to look for these within ourselves in forms much milder than the forms presented to us in the parable.

Second Condition

The second condition is that we must have our spiritual lives in order.

I say 'our spiritual lives' because it is possible that our ordinary everyday lives, physically, or socially, may be somewhat chaotic. St Teresa takes time to describe her own medical difficulties because she suffered from constant noises in her head!

Examples that apply to people in our modern world, as well as ill-health, would be economic worries, security worries, a difficult marriage situation. Another example applicable to everyone nowadays is the all-pervasive blaring into our consciousness of the amoral or immoral values that pervade so much of the media.

These difficulties usually make formal prayer a bit harder, to say the least. But it does not make formal prayer impossible. And this, and so many other concerns in our modern world does not make the grace of contemplation inaccessible. It merely means that we must approach our experience of it in ways different from that of the Carmelite Sisters of St Teresa of Avila, who had the advantage of the peace and tranquillity of their convent enclosure.

Change Resultung from the Prayer of Quiet

So when we have been as faithful as we can to the two conditions referred to above, a change can come in our method of praying. More than that, the change seems to be inevitable – unavoidable.

In the Catholic tradition, and especially in the very popular Ignatian spirituality, we will have been guided in how best to use scripture texts for our meditation, and will have received much good advice. But then, after being faithful to all we have been taught, we will find that it is irksome to have to use scripture texts or any other aid to our praying. This, of course, can be ordinary laziness, an unwillingness to be as methodical as we could and should be in our praying. But if it is not, then at least we can be entering into the Prayer of Quiet.

So the Prayer of Quiet, correctly understood, can be a wordless, and indeed almost unconscious attention to God and to Jesus. Distractions can and will come. But the fact that the intention with which we entered our time of prayer remains unchanged is sufficient to give spiritual value to this time before the Lord, even if we lack consolation and 'job satisfaction'.

Therefore, the fact that, unavoidably, there are moments of distraction in this time must not deflect us from this new way of accepting the special infusion of His very own Life that God is gradually granting to our souls. No matter what our instincts may tell us to the contrary, no matter how much we yearn for our previous 'job satisfaction', we are in fact on the right track. We are not into praying just for the pay-off of 'job satisfaction'. Even if we were, we still do not get it!

We are just going to have to put up with the humiliation of continuing distractions and desolation in prayer.

As I hear often on the radio: 'Terms and conditions apply!'

The 'terms and conditions' have been given to us as guidance for our management of the daily events of our religious lives when we have always been warned by the Church never to forget the existence within us of the tendency towards evil, while at the same time we should equally recognise the existence and potential for good within us.

Each of these tendencies may seem to exist in us in a milder form than sometimes presented in the Scriptures. This may be attributed to the fact that we have been exposed to the Good News within a very Christian background and from our earliest days. As a result, even if these tendencies may in actuality within us be milder than in their form of presentation appropriate for new converts, there is still an urgency for us all to recognise that the level of the New Testament, the level of the early Christians, is still the level demanded from us if we too are to be genuine and successful Christians.

Spiritual Vocabulary

By our very looking here at the ideas of St Teresa, we have thereby to follow her into her spiritual vocabulary of the mansions. We are doing so as we look in more detail at what she has to say about the Prayer of Quiet at the Fourth Mansion level of development.

I have previously mentioned the impact on myself of what Ruth Burrows had to say about 'direct God' when presenting her introduction to the experience of the Fourth Mansion. And if there were on me such a beneficial impact from being introduced to this information, it was natural that I should wonder what more spiritual impact and spiritual benefit might await me in learning about the other mansions which were to follow.

CHAPTER 16

MANSION FIVE

When in the previous chapter I had completed what I had to say about the tremendous change that is involved in the experience of the Fourth Mansion, I had the sense that the main purpose of my writing this book had been achieved. I had, hopefully, either introduced readers to this form of presentation of what Christianity really is or else reviewed for them what they already knew.

If and when we engage in the endeavour of having an intelligent and educated interest in our own spiritual development, and do attain to the Fourth Mansion of spirituality, then to some extent the following stages will take care of themselves in their own good time.

However, I also have the sense that it would leave things hanging if I did not refer even in cursory fashion to the other mansions or levels of spirituality. I do so only to indicate future possibilities for spiritual development, so as to show how the momentum of our transition across the quantum leap into the Fourth Mansion can keep going.

Encouraging

The first feature of entry to this Fifth Mansion which may be of help to us is its message of encouragement: St Teresa tells us that 'most enter these places'.[1] If this be so, then even the bare knowledge that such possibilities of this Mansion exist is both very practical and very encouraging for our spiritual life.

St Teresa's initial purpose had been to write another book about prayer for her Carmelite Sisters, and so it is by offering them descriptions and advice as she went through her teaching on the various stages of prayer that she traces the spiritual development whose possibilities were presented to us in the Parable of the Sower. And one general outline of this part of the development is that 'infused prayer slowly develops through progressing stages, a subsequent growth being usually nothing more than an intensification of the previous one'.[2]

What has happened in the Fourth Mansion has been gradual, transient and almost imperceptible. In the Fifth Mansion, these experiences of God making His Presence known intensify. But changes enter in which distinguish the experience from that of the Fourth Mansion.

> What this prayer lacks in duration, it makes up for not only in intensity but also in the certainty of the divine Presence ... the certitude is such that it can be produced only by God's indwelling ... if this certitude is not present, the experience was not a union with the whole soul with God ... The experi-

---

[1] Rodriguez/Kavenaugh, *St Teresa of Avila*, p. 355.
[2] Thomas Dubay, SM, *Fire Within*, p. 94.

ence is indelible and cannot be forgotten. People who receive this absorption will remember years later the exact time and circumstances in which it occurred.[3]

Prayer of Union

While such an encouragement sounds most attractive, we are warned that such cessation is only for a very short time, a few minutes, 'five, ten or fifteen minutes'.[4]

This intensification of one's prayer brings the person on to reach what St Teresa called 'the Prayer of Quiet'. And the intensification of the Prayer of Quiet brings us to a situation that St Teresa describes as a 'Prayer of Union'.

To make her point about the Fifth Mansion, St Teresa anticipates where she is going to reach in the Sixth and Seventh Mansions. She brings in another example, that of what takes place if there is going to be a betrothal and marriage. This process typically starts with a meeting.

St Teresa says:

The prayer of union does not yet reach the stage of spiritual betrothal. Here below when two people are to be engaged, there is discussion about whether they are alike, whether they love each other, and whether they might meet together so as to become more satisfied with each other. So too, in the case of this union with God, the agree-

[3] Ibid. p. 95.
[4] Ibid. p. 94.

ment has been made and this soul is well informed about the goodness of her spouse ... The soul sees secretly Who her Spouse is that she is going to accept ... The Spouse from that meeting alone leaves her more worthy for the joining of hands, as they say'.[5]

Challenging

But then St Teresa tells us of other essentials of the Fifth Mansion when she describes the special spiritual dynamic that characterises it.

He (God) does not make it impossible for anyone to buy His riches. He is content if each one gives what he has ... But reflect, daughters, that He does not want you to hold on to anything, so that you will be able to enjoy the favour we are speaking of. Whether you have little or much, He wants everything for Himself.'[6]

God will never, in my judgement, grant this favour save to a soul that He takes for His own. He desires that, without its understanding how, it may go forth from this union impressed with His seal. For indeed the soul does no more in this union than does the wax when another impresses a seal on it.[7]

[5] Rodrigue/Kavanagh, *St Teresa of Avila*, ch. 4, p. 355.
[6] Ibid. p. 336.
[7] Ibid. p. 346.

Confrontational

St Teresa then goes on to emphasis the urgency of our being receptive to these gifts of prayer and spiritual development.

> It is God's desire that a favour so great not be given in vain; if a person does not herself benefit, the favour will benefit others ... For since the soul is left with these desires and virtues that were mentioned, it always brings profit to other souls during the time that it continues to live virtuously; and they catch fire from its fire. And even when the soul itself has lost this fire, the inclination to benefit others will remain, and the soul delights in explaining the favours God grants to whoever loves and serves Him.[8]

> I have known persons who had ascended high and had reached this union who were turned back and won over by the devil with his deep cunning and deceit. All hell must join for such a purpose because, as I have often said, in losing one soul of this kind, not only one is lost, but a multitude.[9]

Decision

All the way through her commentary Ruth Burrows has emphasised that St Teresa had a special grace of knowing what was taking place in her soul. This

[8] Ibid. p. 348.
[9] Ibid. p. 356.

grace certainly benefited us all when she was able to speak with such experience and authority on these otherwise mysterious happenings. But Ruth Burrows emphasises that we cannot expect to have this special grace. Therefore, it is a relief when she tells us of her conversation with someone without this special privilege who certainly had experienced the grace of the Fifth Mansion. Ruth Burrows goes on:

> I asked her about the fifth mansion. What did she know of it? After all, she had never known an experience such as marked Teresa's fifth mansion. Had she? No. But was there no experience at all? Her answer was that, looking back – the looking back is most important – she remembers the exact moment which she is sure now corresponds exactly with what Teresa says of her own experience ... There was a 'moment', seemingly so poor and unobtrusive when she was given insight and a choice ... it was, oh, so deeply hidden and yet now she sees it was a most powerful creative grace, an invitation, a call.[10]

Personal Application

My only justification for offering my understanding of the Teresian spirituality is my belief that something like this happened to me, too. When re-reading Ruth Burrows on the Fifth Mansion and wondering if something like that would ever happen to me in the future, I did think of something that had happened in

---

[10] Ruth Burrows, *Interior Castle Explored*, p. 82.

the past which seemed to meet the conditions given.

It was so simple that I had thought that I had never really paid much attention to it, especially since it occurred many years before I ever read about St Teresa's mansions. In a parish where, during recuperation, I had been asked to supply for a short time in the absence of the parish priest, the young assistant priest had organised a catechetical seminar for a few of our neighbouring parishes. But his arrangements were badly upset when speakers that he thought were going to handle that day and the next only gave him a few hours of their time and services. Caught unawares, he managed manfully for the unexpected responsibility of filling in that first day. But at supper time, he declared himself at his wits' end as regards the second day of the seminar. He said nothing more.

I found out later that in view of my being there to recuperate, he did not feel it appropriate to ask my help. And, on my part, I hesitated about offering to help, in case he really did not want it. Eventually I did mention that I was willing to help. The young man was very pleased and greatly relieved. I then had to burn the midnight oil in preparing material for the next day, to develop further what had already been presented. But I managed, and the seminar was declared a success.

Afterwards, when strolling alone that night, I was savouring the good feeling of having been able to help and to have given the catechists useful material. My mind turned momentarily to the Lord in a short prayer of thanksgiving.

Having turned my thoughts in prayer to the young man, and his future success, I immediately found myself with a most preposterous thought in my mind: 'Lord, because of my experience, You don't have to worry about me. With my experience, I can free-wheel successfully and gladly in Your service for the rest of my days as a missionary priest'. As soon as I recognised what the thought was saying, I rejected it out-of-hand, and felt an immediate sense of shame that an idea such as that could arise in me.

But the sense of shame at that incident never really left me.

While I cannot be sure, I have since hoped that my revulsion at that thought and my immediate turning away from it was the kind of incident that St Teresa and Ruth Burrows were referring to and trying to describe. And I recount it here only to illustrate what could be the simplicity of the turning-point in our spiritual lives which occurs as the Fifth Mansion.

Dynamic 'Moment of Decision'

So these three strands all culminate in the decision to commit ourselves to going ahead with acceptance of graces of the Sixth and Seventh Mansions. All of this is what is involved in the grace of the Prayer of Union. Ruth Burrows comments:

> This is the grace of the fifth mansion. It is not a mansion in the sense that it is a place where we are, it is a dynamic moment of decision, offered and accepted, understanding that this acceptance is beyond our power and is a direct effect of God's contact ... The response of the soul at this moment is of such a quality as to be impossible, inconceivable before this stage is reached ... The significance of this is that we can have no knowledge of the fifth mansion until we can look back from the last, from the goal. It can never be deduced from what we

experience or have experienced, from what we feel or what we don't feel.[11]

Perhaps I could now expand my previous summary to read:

God now makes His direct Presence more known than before through encouragement, challenge, confrontation, all culminating in an invitation, a call.

And I could add that if we are still following the pattern outlined for us in the Parable of the Sower, here in this Fifth Mansion we have reached the sixty-fold mark.

We have come a long way in our journey through this interface of the finite and infinite which is our spiritual life.

But there are possibilities for going still further.

---

[11] Ibid. p. 83.

CHAPTER 17

MANSIONS SIX AND SEVEN

The Parable of the Sower jumps from sixty-fold to one hundred-fold. After the arithmetical progression from thirty to sixty, it seemed to me as if it would have been appropriate to have had a ninety-fold and then a hundred-fold. In the parable we do not enjoy that mathematical luxury.

But in St Teresa's treatment of these last two closely-associated mansions, that need is answered for me, even if not by a process of mathematics. St Teresa's purpose was to write especially about the most advanced mystical prayer. To do so, she introduced the terminology of spiritual betrothal and spiritual marriage.

She had so much to say about this that when she got to the culmination, the Sixth and Seventh Mansions, in her treatment of the Sixth Mansion, she wrote eleven chapters. This was her discussion of the first part of the example that she had chosen to use at this point. As completion of what she wanted to say, she then went on to write only four more chapters on the Seventh Mansion. These two mansions represent her descriptions, as best she can give, of what it is like for a soul to experience the heights of mystical prayer

– to have 'reached the Throne Room of His Majesty'.

The Spiritual Marriage

The overall example that she worked out in the whole book was that of a castle, and our purpose was to reach the King in the Throne Room. And our spiritual life with its special kinds of prayer is our reaching this throne-room as the Seventh Mansion. But in these two last chapters, she found it useful to transfer to the example of betrothal and marriage.

The idea of marriage between a man and a woman, creatures each, having any parity with or any application to our relationship with the Infinite God is an idea that could be seen as blasphemous, if it had not originated in God Himself using this image in speaking to His Chosen People. In the Old Testament[1] we read:

'Is she (Israel) not my wife and I her husband?[2]

And:

I will betroth you to Myself for ever, betroth you in lawful wedlock withunfailing devotion and love; I will betroth you to Myself to have and to hold ...[3]

And in the New Testament, we read of St Paul using this same comparison in many places.[4] The most forceful of them is:

[1] Other relevant Old Testament texts: Is. 62:5; 54:4; 62:4; Jer. 2:2; 3:20; Ezek. 16:8.
[2] Hos. 2:2.
[3] Hos. 19–20.
[4] 1 Cor. 7; Col. 3:18; 1 Pet. 3:1–7; Eph. 5:22–33; Aoc. 19:7–9, 21–2.

I arranged for you to marry Christ, so that I might give you away as a chaste virgin to this one husband.[5]

With these for precedents, the term 'spiritual marriage' was a standard and accepted description in spirituality for the upper reaches of the spiritual life and its special prayer. As a result, St Teresa starts her first chapter in this section by writing:

Now the soul is determined to take no other spouse. But the Spouse does not look at the soul's great desires that the betrothal take place, for He still wants it to desire this more and He wants the betrothal to take place at a cost; it is the greatest of blessings. And although everything is small when it comes to paying for this exceptional benefit, I tell you, daughters, that for the soul to endure such delay it needs to have that token or pledge of betrothal that it now has! Oh, God help me, what interior and exterior trials the soul suffers before entering the seventh dwelling place ... unless it has arrived at the seventh dwelling place. For once it has arrived there, the soul fears nothing and is absolutely determined to overcome every obstacle for God.[6]

So St Teresa had a scriptural basis for her conclusion in chapter one of the Seventh Mansion: '....you will understand how important it is for you not to impede your Spouse's celebration of this spiritual marriage with your souls ...'[7]

---

[5] 2 Cor. 11:2.
[6] Rodriguez/Kavenaugh, *St Teresa of Avila*, p. 359.
[7] Ibid. p. 428.

Transforming Union

Nowadays, another term has taken the place of 'spiritual marriage'. It is the term 'transforming union'. This is meant to convey the same information as the example of betrothal and marriage convey to us.

Here I can do no more than confine myself to offering what Ruth Burrows has to say.

> There is a unity between fifth, sixth and seventh mansions. The fifth ushers us into the contemplative life, the life of passionate love; the sixth is the living out of that love, the living of the surrendered heart; the seventh is the perfection of love. The grace of the fifth is the dynamism driving us forward, the sixth is the actual journey, the seventh the goal reached. Here we see what God will do, would we but let him.[8]
>
> The decisive act of choice of the previous mansion opens us to God in a way not possible before, or, more accurately, so enlarges our capacity for him that he is able to give himself in an incomparably fuller measure ... The work of God in us now is consistent because we are consistent in our surrender.
>
> Over and over again, regularly, consistently, in ever increasing measure, divine Love bestows himself, without intermediary of any created, material thing ... We find ourselves profoundly changed and know that this is the work of God ... It will be readily surmised that the sixth mansion covers a very long journey.[9]

[8] Ruth Burrows, *Iterrior Castle Explored*, p. 90.
[9] Ibid. p. 91.

Rather than say that even the experts have reached their limits in their descriptions of this mystical state, I would perhaps be more correct in saying that we all have reached our limits of comprehension unless and until we ourselves personally have experienced the graces of these last final mansions.

There is a disconcerting flatness about the seventh mansion ... These (four) chapters lack the verve characteristic of her writing. The reason is simply that there is nothing that can be said about the seventh mansion ... There is nothing here that she has not already said yet she knows that what she is now talking about is utterly different from everything that has gone before. 'We know that when He appears, we shall be like Him for we shall see Him as He really is' (1 John 3:2). The seventh mansion is this vision of Jesus; not an intellectual insight but a transforming union. The seventh mansion is Jesus, He is living in us and we in Him, the perfection of marriage.[10]

He destined us in love to be His sons through Jesus Christ ... to know the love of Christ which surpasses knowledge, that you may be filled with all the fullness of God.[11]

We become what we are, what we are meant to be ... Only when we are God-filled are we truly human.[12]

After this, there is really no more to be said.[13]

[10] Ibid. p. 110.
[11] Ephesians 1:5, 3:19.
[12] Rodriguez/Kavenaugh, *St Teresa of Avila*, p. 112.
[13] Ibid. p. 110.

I finished previous chapters with a recapitulation and expansion of the summary that I presented at the beginning, and will do so now, so as to finish off the pattern that I started on. But my summary has really very little to add to what has been said before. I would only say:

'God makes His presence (not felt but) known in me as far as He wishes and as far as I have accepted'

Questions and Answers

As regards the theory or model of spirituality of St Teresa of Avila, there is really no more to be said in this brochure-sized summary. Except that, because of the nature of my presentations, some questions still need to be asked – and answered. The questions are:

What about my 'pillar of the church', still living in his remote *barrio*, continuing over the years to 'let God be God in himself' as far as possible'? (And their wives – certainly supports for, and in some cases even sources of, justification for the title I have bestowed!)

What did they know about this theory or model? If obviously they had no direct knowledge of it, what hope had they of attaining its possibilities of spiritual development?

Answers to these questions came to me gradually.

Some time after I myself first learned of the riches of this theory or model, I thought of my memory of my maternal grandfather, an old man of eighty-four when I was still only three or four years of age. The attentions and restrictions under which he, once a very strong and active man, had now to live due to his eighty-four years of age, were very similar to the attention and restrictions of my life as a three- or four-year-old.

Most of the time he had to sit in his armchair, of course, whereas I was always on the move. But apart from that, he and I needed and got almost identical attention, from being helped to dress in the morning, through help with our food at mealtime, until we were helped into bed at night. But whereas everything around me was of intense interest to me, attracting my curiosity, he seemed to be always at peace – and always praying. His rosary beads were constantly in his hands.

I knew all about rosary beads. When at night, after the evening meal, they appeared in the hands of my mother or aunts, it signalled for me the beginnings of an unavoidable endurance exercise! Yet here was my grandfather who, in my view, constantly took this perhaps necessary but certainly unwelcome instrument into his hands when he didn't have to! And then went ahead and used it! Constantly!

When some visitor or well-wisher came into the kitchen where he customarily sat, the rosary beads would disappear into his pocket. But amazingly, they would be brought out again very soon after the visitor had left. That impression of mine as a three-year old and the whole atmosphere of unremitting prayer around my grandfather is still vivid in my mind.

Obviously my grandfather did not have knowledge of the teaching of St Teresa. But after I learned of her teaching and looked around to find examples and applications of it, it dawned on me that he in fact had the grace of the kind of union with God that she wrote about in these final mansions. Here was his 'hundred-fold crop' of the Parable of the Sower. This hundred-fold crop had been discussed in great detail in St Teresa's teaching – yet, without conscious knowledge of the theory, I am very sure that my grandfather was experiencing the actuality!

More Answers

After I remembered that, I began to notice the same atmosphere of constant prayer and the almost tangible presence of God that surrounded some of the invalids and old people I used to visit in their homes.

But, more than that, after some time I realised that in every parish where I had spent sufficient time, I had detected the same atmosphere not just of prayer but of a sense of living in union with God, in people who were not invalids. The pastoral and apostolic activity they were engaged in brought them into constant contact with me. This activity may have been very routine, unobtrusive, even low-grade, as catechists or *barrio capilla* leaders or prayer-group leaders.

My first impression was always of people for whom I was grateful because they were satisfactory in what they were doing for the parish. Average? No! High average! Yes. After all, this is what they had undertaken to do! And for many years, I would have graded them like that!

It was only when time passed and I could see the constancy and dependability and generosity of their humble enough service that I began to realise that this very activity was, in one way, masking for me my appreciation of the depth and intensity of their union with God as they carried out those endeavours. They did not say much. I did not ask much. But gradually I became more and more aware that in all their endeavours, even in the midst of their activity, there was the same kind of peace and serenity as I had first seen in my grandfather.

Petition/Request

I have always prayed that when my time would come, I too would have the same kind of peace and serenity that emanated from this kind of constant union with God. And I trust that whatever I now know about the teaching of St Teresa as presentation of Christianity will be an added help to me now to attain in the future and respond to that same grace – Transforming Union.

CHAPTER 18

NOT KNOWING, KNOWING ABOUT, KNOWING

At the end of the last chapter, I referred to instances of people responding to the grace of God to an extent and with effects which has been described in detail by St Teresa. They did not know the details in the way that I have written about in this book, and yet were spiritually successful. So why write about these details at all?

Knowing 'by Experience'

I had previously made reference to my very strong conviction that I know of my reception of the Grace of Contemplation as described in the chapters on the Fourth Mansion. In the chapter on the Fifth Mansion, I was – or intended to be – much more tentative in anything I had to say about my own experience. And I had nothing of my own experience to offer in the discussion of Mansions Six and Seven.

What does all this amount to?

Even though I have given instances from my own experience, I do so only to illustrate the teaching that I am telling you about.

I know from what Ruth Burrows has written and what I have said in chapter 14 and in chapter 16 that I am thereby taking a risk. So, knowing that it is a risk, I still hope that what I have written will convey to you something of the paradox that I am very much aware of, namely the simplicity and down-right 'ordinariness' of my experiences. This simplicity and 'ordinariness' are all that is needed even when what is supernatural – what is in fact *'direct God'*, as Ruth Burrows states – reaches me.

Two Memories

I can therefore only repeat my intention in writing this book, as I stated it in my introduction. I said that I would describe the two most significant insights concerning my Christianity that I had experienced in the course of my life. As I have already said, I do so purely because of my conviction that what happened to me can happen to others.

And that means you, my unknown reader!

To highlight all that I would like to convey in this book, I call upon two memories of my going swimming. The contrast between them is an example of what it is to add to the sacramental dimension of the knowledge of what are the further possibilities within the Church for our spiritual development, our 'entering into God', even in this world.

To re-visit the first of these memories, I recall the very definite but somewhat vague presence of the 'infinite' Atlantic Ocean on three sides of Ireland. At the same time, I very clearly remember a particular part of it, well known to me from my youth. This is the almost landlocked inlet of Lough Swilly, just a few miles from my home in Ireland. And I fondly remember myself as a youth and then as a young man, being there at my favourite beach.

At that particular spot, I could always see most of Lough Swilly in front of me. The Donegal hills on either side framed its beauty with their own. They also drew one's eye to a little silvery strip at the mouth of the lough where it merged into and imperceptibly became the mighty Atlantic. From my favourite bathing place, I could always see this segment of the Atlantic Ocean as horizon.

Trinity of Waters

Lough Swilly is actually a fjord – one of only two fjords on the island of Ireland – of a length and depth great enough to have been an alternative anchorage during World War One for the British Fleet based in Scapa Flow, after a German submarine had penetrated the Scapa Flow defences. Its great depth as a fjord made it more than adequate for that purpose.

It is therefore as if the 'infinite' Atlantic Ocean had become 'finite' Lough Swilly fjord. And viceversa!

The depth of the fjord made it inaccessible to me. But, near the shore, this depth was stepped down until the depth of five feet or so of what was really the Atlantic water was just perfect for my limited swimming abilities. As far as I was concerned, that was a very satisfactory arrangement, making the Atlantic available to me, putting just as much of the 'infinite' Atlantic as I could manage at my service, for my benefit!

Three bodies of water – yet the same water!

A trinity of waters!

A trinity of waters available to me!

A trinity of waters that I can enter into! Or decline to do so!

Beyond Finite – but not yet Infinite

But now, even if only in my reflection, I go beyond my actual swimming, I think of the unseen depths of the fjord that I know about but was never able to explore. In my imagining those depths, I see a symbol of the potential for us that Scripture and the case study of St Teresa can tell us about the spiritual riches of the Catholic Church.

The body of information about the Church's spiritual riches is much more than I can manage to fully comprehend. But I comprehended some of it more than before when, by an apparent chance, I was introduced by my friend to the teaching of St Teresa. In the same way, the mile-and-a-half of sandy beach was more than I needed to gain access to the water. I chose my favourite spot and usually entered the depths and extensiveness of Lough Swilly, even though that too was more than I could manage. Comprehending more the riches of Catholic doctrine through the writings of St Teresa is my now favoured way of gaining better access to them.

I see the Catholic Church as having something of the same relationship to the total mystery of the Triune God as shallows and then the depths that this limited and almost landlocked Lough Swilly had to the unknown reaches of the Atlantic Ocean. And just as I picked one favourite spot on the beach and entered from there, so there are many ways of getting access to the supernatural graces of God, and I have arbitrarily chosen one in this book.

By being part of Lough Swilly, even if never venturing beyond a depth of five feet, I had thereby some connection with the 'infinity' of the Atlantic Ocean. By having the Catholic Church, I now had available to me an 'interface' between all that was finite in and around me and the infinity of God Himself. Through the Catholic Church, I believe that I am being put in touch with the very real infinity of the life of the Triune God.

Decision – yes

I remember the 'decision' element that had to be present within me for my every swim to take place. Standing at the water's edge on my favourite beach, I was faced with the choice – 'swim now and go home later', or 'don't swim; just go home now' – and its concomitant decision.

When I did take this necessary decision and decided to go swimming, the initial results were not all that pleasant or attractive. I can still remember the cold, cold water inching up the calf of my leg as I advanced deeper and deeper into the waters, following the gentle downward incline of the beach. And always there had to be the unpleasant first plunge!

I never liked that initial coldness. Yet it was unavoidable if I were to get the benefit of the swim that I desired. I had to persevere at enduring it. But shortly after that, I always knew that my persever-ance would pay off. From past experience I knew that when I was fully immersed in the water for just a few moments, the cold would somehow be adjusted to and then forgotten, at least for a short time. Then I would be revelling in my enjoyment of this new element, getting what I could out of it for the short time that I could stand being in it.

So, what was in it for me? What motivated me to go to the trouble of travelling to the beach, getting ready and then enduring the initial cold and the first plunge? By leaving it temporarily and then coming back to it exercised and refreshed after the swim, I always knew that I would be better off than if I had never left my natural element.

The choices and decisions I need for the exercise and then the acquiring of the routine benefits of my Catholic religion can bear a very strong resemblance to all of the above!

Panguil Bay

In the Philippines, how different was my experience of indulging my liking for swimming!

I remember with particular pleasure the opportunity I had to go swimming in the deepish waters at the end of an unused jetty in Panguil Bay in the Southern Philippines. To the north of it I could see a wide swathe of horizon which was the Pacific Ocean within the territorial waters of the Philippines. While it was still horizon, I could see much more of it than the small sliver of horizon I saw so many times at Lough Swilly. This unused jetty in a sheltered part of the bay, made it so very easy for me to reach the enticing clear, greenish, almost tepid tropical waters at its end.

My fellow-Columban who first brought me there was most enthusiastic about the swimming conditions. He brought me out to the end of the jetty – and then I saw the deep water.

There was to be no slow creeping up my leg of the cold waters of my youth! And on entering these tropical waters, no frigid shock. But, poor swimmer that I am, with no experience of diving, I did not very much like the sight of the depth of water at the edge of the jetty. Everything had been easy up until this point. Now was the moment of decision.

The decision was taken for me by virtue of a friendly shove from my fellow-Columban, as he then launched himself into the depths.

I must admit that at that moment I did not particularly like his well-intentioned 'encouragement'. But having come to the surface and having swum a few strokes to get a grip on the jetty supports, I never looked back. In all my experience of swimming in many places, that place was my most-remembered and best-loved.

I use this analogy to represent my two experiences in the progress of my spiritual life.

I can think back to the time in my spiritual life before I had been introduced to the teaching of St Teresa. I now see that time as being like my swimming in Lough Swilly. It was effective and beneficial, but not all that attractive, as I gritted my teeth in my slow progress from my first contact with the water into the safe depths that suited my swimming abilities.

Then came the assistance from my friend who first gave me Ruth Burrow's book. (That assistance was much more gentlemanly than what I got from my confrère in getting to deeper water from my perch at the end of the jetty!). Through that book (and that assistance) came the revelation that I could venture into deeper water spiritually – and having done so, wished to do it more and more!

Mental 'Scaffolding'

The mental picture I have of Our Lord's Ascension is that He graciously – and optimistically – left us to our own devices, to some extent. He expects us to make our moves. When, to the best of our abilities we do so, He will influence what we do in His way and in His time. As a consequence, to guide us through the human-level making of our moves, we have the whole human-level structure of the Church whereby its wisdom is conveyed and made available to us.

But all of the wisdom available has not reached many people!

This means that when, in one way or another, we are presented with this wisdom (as for example in the teaching of St Teresa of Avila), the logistics of conveying this teaching can seem to be like having scaffolding in a building project.

When, in the past, I have had responsibility for building, some of the projects I had to oversee did not need scaffolding. Analogous to that situation are people receiving the graces of contemplation without knowing the details.

But, when for other buildings, I needed scaffolding, I had to buy it, even though I begrudged the money that had to be spent on it. But I knew that we could not manage without it! This is analogous to people who have been taught a little about the teaching of St Teresa. The only way to know is to invest time and effort in looking into the matter. However, we may begrudge the use of such effort. When that is what we do in the spiritual life, our efforts have only brought us as far as 'knowing about'.

But on the other hand, when I had invested in my scaffolding and the building had been completed, all traces of the scaffolding would be gone, with only the results remaining. In the same way, the whole purpose of 'knowing about' teaching like this is that we have the opportunity to go further and reach the point of 'knowing by our own experience'. That is analogous to the usefulness of the 'scaffolding' of our knowledge about things spiritual being tried and proved by direct personal experience.

The very first step in moving from 'not knowing' through to 'knowing about' to 'knowing' is that while, already knowing about the riches of the ordinary sacramental life of the Church, people should also know about the riches of the various spiritualities in the Church.

The teaching of St Teresa of Avila is by no means the only one, but is the one that came my way and that I know best. It does have the power to answer the questions 'What', 'When', 'Why' as regards our spiritual life. But for example, Jesuit spirituality, with its emphasis on discernment, can complement the answers to these three questions with its answers to the other very practical key question 'How'. I have had experience of the benefits of that spirituality, too.

Such knowledge of church spiritualities will enhance even more what is already possible for you as a Catholic. So, it was through my Jesuit-type discernment process that at my retirement from my active missionary work I should be doing God's Will by attempting to put these thoughts on paper in this book.

'*Ad Majorem Dei Gloriam*' – 'For the Greater Glory of God'.

Epilogue

St Teresa used example of a diamond as image of the 'crystal castle'[1] of the King. Jesus used the parable of a 'merchant seeking for the pearls of great price'[2]. From this image we can get many insights.

We moderns, living in an affluent society, can see something approaching the reality of this parable, if we are sufficiently interested in the displays available to us in jewellers' shop windows. But Jesus was speaking to the ordinary people of Palestine. They obviously would have known what a 'pearl of great price' would have been. But at the same time, most of those people probably had never seen one, except perhaps as an occasional glimpse from a distance of the adornments of the 'high and mighty'. Given the undeveloped degree of the scientific knowledge of the times and the low level of general education, there is the very great likelihood that neither did they know much about where pearls came from nor how pearls were formed.

[1] 'Interior Castle Explored' p. 6.
[2] Matt. 13:45–6.

Most people now know about the extraordinary way in which pearls are formed in oysters.

Oysters are living organisms, shellfish which can be found in abundance especially in tropical waters. Our modern scientists have found the actual cause of pearls forming. Sometimes a tiny grain of sand gets into an oyster in its natural state. Because it is an irritant, the living organism of the oyster, in self-protection, secretes a fluid which isolates the irritating grain of sand. The fluid hardens into being the material that we call 'pearl'. The end-product is much sought-after.

In the natural state, this occurs only in some oysters. Because of this knowledge now utilised by skilled technicians, there are industries for producing pearls. The technicians introduce an irritant into every oyster. This is done by first cultivating oyster-beds in easily accessible waters, then taking the oysters temporarily from their seabed home, inserting a suitable piece of grit, and returning them to the seabed. As a result of this 'dynamic', in due course, the people who do this preparation work have an opportunity to harvest the oysters and find in each of them the profitable results which are cultured pearls that can be sold.

Pearls, even cultured pearls, have such beauty that they are highly valued. But this beauty would not have come into existence had it not been not for the irritant of the grain of sand.

Application

Could we see the state of Adam and Eve in the idyllic conditions of the Garden of Eden as being like our natural pearls in their native habitat, undisturbed by modern industry? Could we see Original Sin as an irritant purposefully introduced into Adam and Eve by the greatest of all Technicians, God Himself? Could we see ourselves as the multiplication by that same Technician into many Adams and Eves, just as industry has multiplied oysters for the production of pearls? Could we see Original Sin as an irritant forcing our spirits, in self-protection, to counteract the effects of this irritant? Can we see the Suffering Jesus in His Passion and Death as the essential source of Salvation, a divine salve secreted against the effects of the irritant grain of sand which is Original Sin? Could we accept the same process as going on in our persons, 'culturing' a new, most valuable product, the Kingdom of Heaven?

Mankind can therefore be likened to the oyster, valuable enough in itself. But the irritation of Original Sin was introduced by the Hand of God. With His specialised knowledge of His own plans, He is in fact knowingly and wilfully committed to producing the 'cultured pearls' of the beauty of our souls – the Kingdom of God. The insights of St Teresa are now like the specialised knowledge that the technicians of this industry now have from their own experience.

Application to me

The reality of what was symbolised in the pearl of the parable is to be found in the depths of my consciousness. It is in these depths that I make my crucial decisions. Decisions stemming from what I know about Jesus and myself. Decisions about what I know of what is finite and infinite, and what I can learn about them even in this world. Decisions, unavoidable because of the irritant of Original Sin. All of these decisions about accepting what is on offer from God!

The process of our lives can then be seen as spiritual development. This irritant of Original Sin can then cause my individual *'pearl of great price'* to come slowly into being as my real self, as my transforming union with God develops.

So, in view of this added knowledge, we can differentiate the parable of the pearl of great price from the event described in the apparently similar parable, that of finding by chance a treasure in a field.[3] This preceding parable tells of the treasure, our Christianity, with which we have been gifted. Now this parable of 'the pearl of great price' tells us that this treasure is to be cared for by being managed and developed in the way that an industrious businessman takes care of his business Our business happens to be simultaneously the greater glory of God, and our own eternal benefit. Assisted by the knowledge imparted by St Teresa, we have all the right conditions for the development of becoming more and more 'christed' – the Old English form of 'christened'.

In the interface between the finite that I am and the Infinite that God is, Christian transition within me is possible. *Even in this world!*

---

[3] Matt. 13:44.